STUDIES IN CULTURE AND COMMUNICATION
General Editor: John Fiske

UNDERSTANDING
TELEVISION

IN THE SAME SERIES

# UNDERSTANDING TELEVISION

*Edited by*

# Andrew Goodwin

*and*

# Garry Whannel

ROUTLEDGE • LONDON AND NEW YORK

First published 1990
by Routledge
11 New Fetter Lane, London EC4P 4EE

Simultaneously published in the USA and Canada
by Routledge
a division of Routledge, Chapman and Hall, Inc.
29 West 35th Street, New York, NY 10001

Set in 10/12 Garamond by Columns of Reading
Printed in Great Britain by Richard Clay Ltd, Bungay, Suffolk

British Library Cataloguing in Publication Data
Understanding television. – (Studies in Culture and Communication)
 1. Great Britain. Role of television
 I. Goodwin, Andrew II. Whannel, Garry III. Series
 302.2'345

Library of Congress Cataloging in Publication Data
Understanding television / edited by Andrew Goodwin and Garry Whannel.
 p.  cm.—(Studies in culture and communication)
 Includes bibliographical references.
 1.  Television broadcasting.  I. Goodwin, Andrew, 1956- .
 II. Whannel, Garry.  III. Series.
 PN1992.5.U48 1900
 384.55—dc20     89–10954

ISBN 0–415–01671–1
    0–415–01672–X (pbk)

# CONTENTS

# LIST OF
# CONTRIBUTORS

Mick Bowes is Vice Principal of Chelmsford Adult Education Institute and is actively involved in a number of community media projects.

Rosalind Brunt teaches Mass Communication and Women's Studies at Sheffield City Polytechnic. She is also the Director of the Centre for Popular Culture, based at the Polytechnic, and is on the editorial board of *Marxism Today*.

Verina Glaessner is a freelance journalist and critic.

Andrew Goodwin is a lecturer in the Department of Broadcast Communication Arts, San Francisco State University.

Patrick Hughes teaches Communications and Journalism at Warrnambool Institute of Advanced Education in Australia.

Paul Kerr is a producer on Channel Four's weekly series *The Media Show*.

Justin Lewis teaches at the Department of Communications at the University of Massachussets.

Michael O'Shaughnessy is a lecturer in Film and TV Studies at Leicester Polytechnic.

Richard Paterson is the Head of the Television Unit at the British Film Institute.

Paddy Scannell is a senior lecturer at the Polytechnic of Central London and an editor of the journal *Media, Culture and Society*.

John Tulloch is Principal Lecturer in Journalism in the Faculty of Communication, Polytechnic of Central London.

Garry Whannel is a writer and researcher specializing in television and sport.

# GENERAL EDITOR'S PREFACE

This series of books on different aspects of communication is designed to meet the needs of the growing number of students coming to study this subject for the first time. The authors are experienced teachers or lecturers who are committed to bridging the gap between the huge body of research available to the more advanced student, and what the new student actually needs to get him started on his studies.

Probably the most characteristic feature of communication is its diversity: it ranges from the mass media and popular culture, through language to individual and social behaviour. But it identifies links and a coherence within this diversity. The series will reflect the structure of its subject. Some books will be general, basic works that seek to establish theories and methods of study applicable to a wide range of material; others will apply these theories and methods to the study of one particular topic. But even these topic-centred books will relate to each other, as well as to the more general ones. One particular topic, such as advertising or news or language, can only be understood as an example of communication when it is related to, and differentiated from, all the other topics that go to make up this diverse subject.

The series, then, has two main aims, both closely connected. The first is to introduce readers to the most important results of contemporary research into communication together with the theories that seek to explain it. The second is to equip them with appropriate methods of study and investigation which they will be able to apply directly to their everyday experience of communication.

If readers can write better essays, produce better projects and pass more exams as a result of reading these books I shall be very satisfied; but if they gain a new insight into how communication shapes and informs our social life, how it articulates and creates our experience of industrial society, then I shall be delighted. Communication is too often taken for granted when it should be taken to pieces.

John Fiske

# INTRODUCTION
## *Andrew Goodwin* and *Garry Whannel*

The study of television in our society takes place at poles that are almost comic in their extremes. In our daily lives, television is constantly 'studied' – in the popular press, on buses and trains, in our kitchens and living rooms, on the radio, and in every sphere of our lives where conversation occurs. This study of television is usually anecdotal, sometimes self-conscious, and nearly always atheoretical. At the other extreme there has grown up over the last two decades a body of academic theories and concepts that can be applied to television. Dozens of books and journals now publish analyses of television deriving from sociology, Marxism, semiotics, structuralism, feminism, linguistics, psychoanalysis, and postmodern theory. In the yawning gap between these two kinds of study, TV criticism in newspapers and magazines is the only routinely published analysis of television. Yet that work remains little more than gossip in five syllables, or, in the case of the tabloids, monosyllabic gossip. TV criticism offers little help in understanding television as long as it is primarily a forum for writers to air personal opinions, unhindered by any need to grasp twentieth-century cultural theory.

Meanwhile, teachers and students pick up the threads of these analyses (from 'did you hear what Sheila said to Rick last night?' to 'is *Brookside* a realist text?') and attempt to cope with the fact that there is so little published material about television that is accessible to students who are relative strangers in the world of theory and the practice of analysing popular culture. It is for those students and teachers that this book is written. It arose from the experience that all the contributors share, of teaching about television at introductory levels, in adult education and to undergraduates. Many of the authors taught on the University of

London's Certificate in Television Studies, started by the Department of Extra-Mural Studies in 1978. Those of us who taught (and still teach) these classes were struck by the absence of any single text that could be used to introduce new students to the history, social context, and textual interpretation of television.

This book attempts to fulfil that role, by gathering together short, accessible essays that encapsulate the main issues at stake in contemporary British television. In doing this, the authors all draw on a large body of theory and empirical work developed over the last twenty years.

The study of television has its genesis in a number of disciplines (see Cook and Hillier 1976). As early as the 1940s sociologists had begun to ponder the effects of the new medium – this was especially so in the United States, where the analysis of new media was less hindered than in Europe by assumptions about the aesthetic superiority of older cultural forms. Sociology has continued to study television, lodging a particular stake in the analysis of its audience, through 'effects' studies, the 'uses and gratifications' school of research, and later attempts to refine these approaches and perhaps even combine them with ideas from other text-based kinds of work.

The other early input into television study was literary and cultural criticism. By the 1950s a diverse body of work had grown up that is often collected under the rubric 'cultural pessimism', due to the largely negative interpretations produced in most of its studies, which tended to see mass culture (including television) as a problem. In the USA this school united Marxists aligned with the Frankfurt School with neo-conservatives like Dwight MacDonald and Daniel Bell. (It lives on in the work of contemporary critics of television, such as Neil Postman and Jerry Mander.) In Britain cultural pessimism was mainly associated with the work of literary critic F. R. Leavis, and the Leavisites, who expended a lot of energy in the pursuit of 'discrimination' – that is, the ability to sort the wheat from chaff, to make cultural judgements informed by the 'correct' aesthetic and moral criteria.

In Britain in the 1970s the study of television underwent some dramatic changes, and it is this shift that forms the conceptual underpinning of this book. Drawing on a vast body of cultural theory (much of it imported from the Continent), television studies (like film studies) began to engage with concepts which subsumed the questions of personal taste discussed in TV criticism and which went beyond the cultivation of 'discrimination'. The study of the social context of television institutions was developed more fully in some early sociological (Burns 1977), historical (Williams 1974; Briggs 1979), and political economic (Murdock and Golding 1977; Garnham 1978) work on the medium. This analysis was framed by new, broader questions about ideology, economic power, and social legitimation. The study of the television audience was wrenched from an obsession with 'effects' and became more concerned with the altogether more complex question of how audiences make meanings out of TV 'texts' (Fiske and Hartley 1979; Hall 1980). The use of the word 'text', along with terms like 'code' and 'mode of address', derived from the introduction of a new field of study – semiotics, the science of signs. If semiotics didn't magically 'solve' the problem of interpretation by offering a complete science of meaning, it certainly did bring with it tools for the analysis of culture that were considerably more refined and relevant than those of literary criticism or sociology.

This development of media theory and cultural analysis produced new interpretations of cinema, pop music, youth subcultures, fashion, advertising, and sport. And it transformed the study of television. Many of the new concepts in television studies derived from or owed something to the theoretical work done in film studies. And so it was no surprise to find that the British Film Institute played an important role in the development of the study of television, through conferences, publications, and involvement in teaching. The Society for Education in Film and Television (SEFT) was another focus for the cross-fertilization of cinema and TV, and their journals *Screen* and *Screen Education* published much of the important work that constituted the 'new' analysis of TV.

A number of institutions of higher education also contributed to this new approach. Birmingham University's Centre for Contemporary Cultural Studies (under the directorship of Richard Hoggart, and then Stuart Hall) played a pioneering role in introducing theoretical approaches from France, Italy, and Germany to British audiences. Its journal *Working Papers in Cultural Studies* published some important contributions to TV theory, including Umberto Eco's seminal attempt to begin the semiotic study of TV, 'Towards a semiotic inquiry into the television message'. Other institutions (such as the School of Communication at the Polytechnic of Central London and Leicester University's Centre for Mass Communication Research) taught about television from these new critical perspectives.

Thereafter the study of television and the media developed largely in higher education, and in many cases only at postgraduate level. In this rarefied atmosphere the attempt to offer popular or accessible analysis was usually of secondary concern. The difficult business of making this material more accessible was often left to hard-pressed teachers who boned up on the latest theories in *Screen*, or on a BFI weekend school, and then attempted to translate them back into language that could be understood by the uninitiated. Media theory was hard to tackle, both because its terms could often seem obfuscating, and because it was genuinely and necessarily complex. Its meaning could not be understood in relation to theories of ideology without engaging some extremely complicated debates. Its texts could not be unpacked without the resort to some difficult new methodologies. New terms entered the lexicon of the scholar of television: genre, mode of address, metaphor, metonymy, realism, naturalism, ideology, hegemony, code, convention, polysemy . . . and so on. (One task of this book is to explain some of these terms to students new to this field.)

There is no doubt that the task of making this body of work accessible is a difficult one. This has been a special problem for those of us teaching in adult education. But if academics are correct to complain that most TV critics are less interested in television than they are in their own writing careers, it must also be said that the academy could do a little more to popularize itself. Outside the United Kingdom it isn't so unusual for theorists to publish TV and cultural criticism in newspapers and popular publications. In Britain, the gulf between the theoretical and the accessible is especially wide. Apart from occasional contributions to the pages of the *Listener*, *New Socialist*, *Marxism Today*, and the *New Statesman and Society* (where a number of our contributors write from time to time), most TV studies analysis has gone on in relatively obscure journals. Despite the efforts of the BFI and others (the Comedia publishing house, for instance – see Root 1986) to make accessible texts and new teaching materials available, this book is one of the first introductory texts about television that offers a broad view of institutions, texts, and audiences (see also Masterman 1985; Clarke 1987; Alvarado, Gutch, and Wollen 1987).

One problem that might explain the delay in 'cashing in' the advances of the 1970s is that those developments remain extremely uneven. They range from relatively prosaic efforts to undertake sociological studies of television through to wordy engagements with the outer conceptual reaches of psychoanalytic theory. And many of these theoretical advances remain as yet unconsolidated. One perhaps necessary side-effect of the explosion of cultural theory in the 1970s was a tendency for media analysis to latch onto new ideas in an almost ephemeral fashion that resembled television more closely than scholarship. Students of television grappled with the implications of, say, the structuralist analysis of Louis

4

Althusser . . . only to discover that the academy went 'poststructuralist' that very same week. New theories of ideology and culture often seemed to be uncovered, developed, critiqued, and abandoned within a matter of months. (One explanation for this lies in the poverty of British theory, which often latched onto developments abroad very late, only to discover that they were already out of date.)

We exaggerate this 1970s trend in order to make a serious point: that one effect of this emphasis on new theory was the premature abandonment of many potentially fruitful concepts and paradigms. One only has to think of the way in which the ideas of the German Marxists of the Frankfurt School were first rediscovered, then parodied and critiqued (as parody), and finally discarded. In the process, a number of important insights were lost, and any attempt to re-engage with them could quickly be dismissed as thoroughly *passé* in the fast-moving world of 1970s media theory.

A great deal of 1970s analysis of television and the media has yet to be fully worked through. There is the question not only of those paradigms that might usefully be re-evaluated, but also the problem of inadequate theoretical projects which remain abandoned by the analytical roadside, like clapped-out old cars. Their breakdown has yet to be fully understood. The debate about 'realism' is one such abandoned rust-bucket. In the 1970s the theoretical air crackled with concepts that derived from Marxism, feminism, psychoanalysis, and cinematic and literary theory, and academic journals like *Screen* and *Framework* published numerous articles analysing television in these terms. Eventually this work collapsed under the weight of its own theoreticism and the debate about realism and modernism was simply abandoned in favour of a new (and apparently *unrelated*) discussion about 'post-modernism', which takes place as though the early 1970s positions never existed.

One problem for 1970s work was an understandable infatuation with theory at the expense of empirical analysis, and a related tendency (clearly determined by the politics of academia) to fetishize 'originality'. An original theory was often more exciting and prestigious than an explanatory one. It is generally agreed that one problem in evaluating competing theories developed in the 1970s was the lack of concrete analysis involved in merely applying theories to texts and thus producing dozens of (sometimes contradictory) 'readings'.

In the 1980s there was a tendency to move back towards the empirical; towards testing out critical debates through an engagement with the site of production (Feuer, Kerr, and Vahimagi 1984; Ellis

1982); towards a testing out of critical theories via closer readings of the text (see Newcomb 1987; Masterman 1985); and towards a testing out of textual readings through a study of actual audiences (see Hobson 1982; Ang 1985; Lewis 1985; and Morley 1986). There has also been a related interest and commitment to the *popular*. That is to say, where theory in the 1970s often looked at popular television to discover whether or not it measured up to certain pre-given theoretical and political criteria, the 1980s have seen a shift towards taking the popular on its own terms, and beginning with actual public taste cultures (in order to understand them better), rather than abstract theories (Bennett *et al*. 1981; Dyer 1981 and 1985). This period has thus seen a shift from a focus on 'serious' television (drama, documentary, news, current affairs) to popular entertainment forms (soap opera, situation comedy, pop music video, sport, game show and so on). This approach has its advantages (and does, after all, derive from a theory – a paradigm built on the writings of Antonio Gramsci), but is also has its detractors (see Gardner and Shepherd 1984; Williamson, 1986).

A further and more difficult shift in 1980s approaches emerged out of a perceived change in television itself. This was the debate about postmodernism. This term is notoriously difficult to pin down, but can be summarized in this context as a concern with a number of ways in which contemporary television is seen to defy the old modes of analysis deriving from literary and cinematic theory. Critics point to programmes like *Miami Vice*, *Late Night With David Letterman*, *The Singing Detective*, and *Max Headroom*, and to new forms and services like music video and MTV, as examples of television that is qualitatively different from the texts of the 1970s (see Gitlin 1987; Grossberg 1987). While these critics certainly can't be said to agree among themselves, the common themes in such analyses are a concern for television's recent incorporation of *avant-garde*/modernist devices, its 'flatness' and emphasis on surface style, its abandonment of traditional narrative; and its tendency to be self-reflexive and about itself (rather than a mediation between itself and an extrinsic 'reality'). Many critics now argue that this postmodern aesthetic requires new ways of 'reading' and understanding television.

Clearly a further important trend (and perhaps a related one) in the 1980s concerns not the text–reader relation addressed by postmodern critics, but the text–institution relation that is radically altered by the growing deregulation of television, on both sides of the Atlantic. The 1986 Peacock Report on broadcasting offered a challenge to British assumptions about the organization of television as a public service. In the context of British television this has meant a radical questioning of the assumptions that analysts once took for granted. It has also meant an engagement with the proliferation of sites of distribution, as television becomes available not as a text transmitted by a national duopoly, but as a product available through a multiplicity of marketplace sources – home video and cable and satellite TV now supplement the public service institutions of television.

In attempting to address these debates, this book is designed to provide readers with a basis for *working forward* into the 1980s reformulations. That is to say, it doesn't assume that the theoretical work of the 1970s can be abandoned in favour of the empirical, the popular, or the postmodern. It assumes that the new emphases can only be understood through an engagement with concepts such as ideology, hegemony, and bias, and through an understanding of how television mediates the social relations of gender, race, and class.

Because this is primarily an *introductory* text, we have stressed accessibility over complexity, in an effort to provide an overview that readers can build upon and develop at greater levels of sophistication in their own study, reading, and analysis. Each chapter thus surveys a debate or *genre* as widely and clearly as possible, providing a suggested follow-up reading list of three or four key texts, in addition to other references. There is of course no attempt to unify the contributions into a seamless position – there are distinctly different approaches underlying some of the contributions. Nor is there any attempt to suggest that these introductory essays constitute a theoretically integrated approach to television analysis. The essays here present very different histories – of institutions and policies, of audience research and programming. Paddy Scannell's account of the development of public service broadcasting is in marked contrast, for instance, to John Tulloch's historical engagement with race and British broadcasting. Patrick Hughes offers a different perspective again on the post-broadcasting technologies, as does Richard Paterson in his discussion of the TV schedule – although either of them might easily be integrated with Scannell's defence of public service. Andrew Goodwin's account of TV news raises questions of audience consumption that are taken up more fully by Justin Lewis in his account of the audience.

Similarly, the different approaches to texts present sometimes complementary and sometimes widely divergent analyses. Goodwin's essay on TV news raises questions about ideology and television from within a paradigm that has generally been dominated by sociological content analysis. Rosalind Brunt's chapter, on the other hand, is intended to introduce other techniques of text analysis developed over the last fifteen years or so. And these ideas are then taken up by a number of our contributors in a debate that is still framed (in our view) by the political questions opened up in Michael O'Shaughnessy's piece on the concept of hegemony. Paul Kerr's analysis of the drama-documentary debate, Verina Glaessner's discussion of soap opera, Garry Whannel's analysis of sports and quizzes, and Mick Bowes' essay on situation comedy each consider different aspects of the politics of popular television programming.

We haven't made the common division between historical, institutional, and textual analysis in our ordering of the essays, since many of our contributors specifically refuse such separations. (Both Kerr and Whannel, for instance, have as much to say about institutions as they do about programming.) Neither have we considered the notion of genre in the abstract – although the attempt to understand the rules and conventions that govern our understanding of the different parts of the TV schedule is certainly written in to many of the essays. Perhaps most interesting of all the questions raised in that debate is the issue of informational versus entertainment programming, and how each makes its own very different truth claims. Reading through the pieces that follow, we hope that our readers will notice both the clashes and connections between television's factual and fictional discourses: in its efforts to mediate political conflict in news (Goodwin), drama-documentary (Kerr), and sitcom (Bowes), for instances; or in the role of both factual and fictional 'personalities' discussed by Brunt, O'Shaughnessy, and Whannel.

Making these connections involves an engagement with the politics of television that will, we hope, take you beyond the remit of this book. As this introduction has tried to indicate, the task of under-standing television in the 1990s is to tackle the awkward relationship between the new emphases of empirical, populist, and postmodern studies in the 1980s and the discovery of theory that occurred in the preceding decade.

## References

Alvarado, M., Gutch, R., and Wollen, T., *Learning the Media*, London: Macmillan, 1987.
Ang, I., *Watching Dallas*, London: Methuen, 1985.
Bennett, T. *et al.* (eds), *Popular Television and Film*, London: British Film Institute, 1981.

Briggs, A., *The History of Broadcasting in the United Kingdom*, vol. 4: *Sound and Vision*, Oxford: Oxford University Press, 1979.

Burns, T., *The BBC: Public Institution and Private World*, London: Macmillan, 1977.

Clarke, M., *Teaching Popular Television*, London: Heinemann, 1987.

Cook, J. and Hillier, J., *The Growth of Film and Television Studies, 1960–75*, London: British Film Institute, 1976.

Dyer, R. (ed.), *Coronation Street*, London: British Film Institute, 1981.

Dyer, R., 'Taking popular television seriously', in D. Lusted and P. Drummond (eds), *TV and Schooling*, London: British Film Institute, 1985.

Eco, U., 'Towards a semiotic inquiry into the television message', *Working Papers in Cultural Studies*, no. 3, Birmingham: Centre for Contemporary Cultural Studies, University of Birmingham, 1972.

Ellis, J., *Visible Fictions*, London: Routledge & Kegan Paul, 1982.

Feuer, J., Kerr, P., and Vahimagi, T., *MTM: 'Quality Television'*, London: British Film Institute, 1984.

Fiske, J. and Hartley, J., *Reading Television*, London: Methuen, 1979.

Gardner, C. and Shepherd, J., 'Transforming television – part one, the limits of Left policy', *Screen*, vol. 25, no. 2 (1984).

Garnham, N., *Structures of Television*, London: British Film Institute, 1978.

Gitlin, T., 'Car commercials and *Miami Vice*: we build excitement', in Gitlin (ed.), *Watching Television*, New York: Pantheon, 1987.

Grossberg, L., 'The in-difference of television', *Screen*, vol. 28, no. 2 (1987).

Hall, S., 'Encoding and decoding in television discourse', in S. Hall, D. Hobson, A. Lowe and P. Willis (eds), *Culture, Media, Language*, London: Hutchinson, 1980.

Hobson, D., *Crossroads: Drama of a Soap Opera*, London: Methuen, 1982.

Lewis, J., 'Decoding TV news', in P. Drummond and R. Paterson (eds), *Television in Transition*, London: British Film Institute, 1985.

Masterman, L. (ed.), *Television Mythologies: Stars, Shows and Signs*, London: Comedia, 1985.

Morley, D., *Family Television: Cultural Power and Domestic Leisure*, London: Comedia, 1986.

Murdock, G. and Golding, P., 'Capitalism, communications and class relations', in J. Curran, M. Gurevitch, and J. Woollacott (eds), *Mass Communication and Society*, London: Edward Arnold, 1977.

Newcomb, H. (ed.), *Television: The Critical View*, Oxford: Oxford University Press, 1987.

Root, J., *Open The Box: About Television*, London: Comedia, 1986.

Williams, R., *Television: Technology and Cultural Form*, London: Fontana, 1974.

Williamson, J., 'The problems with being popular' in *New Socialist*, no. 41 (September 1986).

For a guide to further reading see the *Television Studies Bibliography*, compiled by Andrew Goodwin, available from BFI Education, 21 Stephen Street, London W1P 1PL.

# 1 PUBLIC SERVICE BROADCASTING: THE HISTORY OF A CONCEPT

*Paddy Scannell*

It is well known that broadcasting in Britain is based on the principle of public service, though what exactly that means, on close inspection, can prove elusive. The last parliamentary committee to report on broadcasting – the 1986 Peacock Committee – noted that it had experienced some difficulty in obtaining a definition of the principle from the broadcasters themselves. A quarter of a century earlier, the members of the Pilkington Committee on broadcasting were told by the chairman of the BBC's Board of Governors that it was no use trying to define good broadcasting – one recognized it. Maybe. Yet for the sake of reasonable discussion of the relevance or otherwise of public service broadcasting today it is worth trying to pin down the characteristics that define the British system. A useful starting point is to distinguish between public service as a responsibility delegated to broadcasting authorities by the state, and the manner in which the broadcasting authorities have interpreted that responsibility and tried to discharge it.

Government intervention to regulate broadcasting has been, in many cases, the outcome of wavelength scarcity and problems of financing. The portion of the electromagnetic spectrum suitable for broadcasting is limited and governments have had to assume responsibility for negotiating international agreements about wavelength allocations to particular countries as well as deciding how to parcel out the wavelengths available in their own country amongst the competing claims of broadcasting and those of the armed forces, merchant shipping, emergency services, telecommunications, and so on. The problem of financing arises because it is not immediately obvious how people are to be made to pay for a broadcast service. Most forms of culture and entertainment are funded by the box-office mechanism – people pay to enter a special place to enjoy a play, concert, film, or whatever. But radio and television are enjoyed in people's homes and appear as natural resources available, at the turn of a switch, like gas, water, or electricity. The two means of financing broadcasting in universal use, until recently, have been either a form of annual taxation on the owners of receiving sets (the licence fee), or advertising.

The British solution, back in the early 1920s, was the creation of a single company, the British Broadcasting Company, licensed to broadcast by the Post Office and financed by an annual licence fee charged on all households with a wireless. How the concept of public service came to be grafted onto what were originally a set of *ad hoc*, practical arrangements and the shifting terms of debate about what it has meant, can best be traced through the various committees on broadcasting set up by successive governments from the beginning through to the present. These committees, usually known by the name of their chairmen, have been given the task of reporting to Parliament on the conduct of the broadcasters, the general nature of the service provided, and its possible future development. They have been the means whereby Parliament has kept an eye on the activities of those to whom it has delegated responsibility for providing broadcast services in this country.

The very first broadcasting committee, set up by the Post Office in 1923 under the chairmanship of Major-General Sir Frederick Sykes, was asked to consider broadcasting in all its aspects and the future uses to which it might be put. In the minuted proceedings of this committee and its report we find the earliest attempts to formulate what the general purposes of broadcasting should be. A crucial move was the definition of broadcasting as 'a public utility' whose future should be discussed as such.

> The wavebands available in any country must be regarded as a valuable form of public property; and the right to use them for any purpose should be given after full and careful consideration. Those which are assigned to any particular interest should be subject to the safeguards necessary to protect the public interest in the future. (Sykes 1923: 11)

Bearing in mind the cheapness and convenience of radio, and its social and political possibilities ('as great as any technical attainment of our generation'), the committee judged that 'the control of such a potential power over public opinion and the life of the nation ought to remain with

12

the state' (Sykes 1923: 15). The operation of so important a national service ought not to be allowed to become an unrestricted commercial monopoly.

The report rejected direct government control of broadcasting. Instead, it argued, indirect control should be operated through the licence which by law must be obtained from the Post Office for the establishment of any broadcasting station. The terms of the licence would specify the general responsibilities of the broadcasters and hold them answerable for the conduct of the service to that state department.

Thus the definition of broadcasting as a public utility, and the mandate to develop it as a national service in the public interest, came from the state. The interpretation of that definition, the effort to realize its meaning in the development of a broadcasting service guided by considerations of a national service and the public interest, came from the broadcasters and above all from John Reith, the managing director of the British Broadcasting Company from 1923 to 1926, and the first Director-General of the British Broadcasting Corporation from 1927 to 1938. The Sykes Committee had made only short-term recommendations about the development of a broadcasting service and the BBC had been granted a licence to broadcast for only two more years. The Crawford Committee was set up in 1925 to establish guidelines for the future of broadcasting on a more long-term basis. Reith was invited by the committee to present it with a statement of his views about the scope and conduct of broadcasting and he did so in a memorandum which he wrote as an impartial statement, presented in the interests of broadcasting not the British Broadcasting Company, and intended to show the desirability of the conduct of broadcasting as a public service.

In Reith's brief and trenchant manifesto for a public service broadcasting system there was an overriding concern for the maintenance of high standards and a unified policy towards the whole of the service supplied. The service must not be used for entertainment purposes alone. Broadcasting had a responsibility to bring into the greatest possible number of homes in the fullest degree all that was best in every department of human knowledge, endeavour, and achievement. The preservation of a high moral tone – the avoidance of the vulgar and the hurtful – was of paramount importance. Broadcasting should give a lead to public taste rather than pander to it: 'He who prides himself on giving what he thinks the public wants is often creating a fictitious demand for lower standards which he himself will then satisfy' (Reith 1925: 3). Broadcasting had an educative role and the broadcasters had developed contacts with the great educational movements and institutions of the day in order to develop the use of the medium of radio to foster the spread of knowledge.

Here we find a cogent advocacy of public service as a cultural, moral, and educative force for the improvement of knowledge, taste, and manners, and this has become one of the main ways in which the concept is understood. But radio, as Reith was well aware, had a social and political function too. As a national service, broadcasting might bring together all classes of the population. It could prove to be a powerful means of promoting social unity particularly through the live relay of those national ceremonies and functions – Reith cited the speech by George V when opening the British Empire Exhibition: the first time the king had been heard on radio – which had the effect, as he put it, of 'making the nation as one man' (Reith 1925: 4). By providing a common access for all to a wide range of public events and ceremonies – a royal wedding, the FA Cup Final, the last night of the Proms, for example – broadcasting would act as a kind of social cement binding people together in the shared idioms of a public, corporate, national life.

But, more than this, broadcasting had an immense potential for helping in the creation of an informed and enlightened democracy. It enabled men and women to take an interest in many things from which they had previously been excluded. On any great public issue of the day radio could provide both the facts of the matter and the arguments for and against. Reith had a vision of the emergence of 'a new and mighty weight of public opinion' with people now enabled by radio to make up their own minds where previously they had to accept 'the dictated and partial versions of others' (Reith 1925: 4). The restrictive attitude of the Post Office which, at the time, had forbidden the BBC to deal with any matters of public controversy, was severely restricting the development of this side of broadcasting, and Reith bitterly denounced the shackles imposed on radio's treatment of news and politics. Only when freed from such chains would broadcasting be able to realize one of its chief functions. The concept of public service, in Reith's mind, had, as a core element, an ideal of broadcasting's role in the formation of an informed and reasoned public opinion as an essential part of the political process in a mass democratic society.

Finally, Reith argued strongly for continued 'unity of control' in broadcasting – that is, for the maintenance of the BBC's monopoly of broadcasting in the United Kingdom. The monopoly granted to the BBC in 1922 was merely for the administrative convenience of the Post Office –

it found it easier to deal with one licensed broadcasting service than several. At first there had been a considerable outcry (particularly from the popular press) against this 'trade monopoly' as a restrictive practice which inhibited the development of a range of competing programme services for listeners to choose from. But Reith defended what he later called the 'brute force of monopoly' as the essential means of guaranteeing the BBC's ability to develop as a public service in the national interest. The monopoly was, Reith argued, the best means of sorting out a technically efficient and economical system of broadcasting for the whole population − and universal availability was the cornerstone of the creation of a truly national service in the public interest. Second, unity of control was essential ethically in order that 'one general policy may be maintained throughout the country and definite standards promulgated' (Reith 1925: 10).

Reith favoured changing the status of the BBC from a company in the private sector, set up originally in the interests of the British radio industry, to a corporation in the public sector under the authority of the state, because he believed it would give broadcasting a greater degree of freedom and independence in the pursuit of the ideals of public service. On the one hand it was necessary to be freed from commercial pressures. If radio continued to be part of a profit-oriented industry then the programme service would be influenced by commercial considerations and the need to appeal to popular demand. Entertainment, a legitimate aim of broadcasting, would become a paramount consideration to the detriment of other kinds of programming with a more educative or culturally improving aim. On the other hand, broadcasting needed to be free of interference and pressure from the state in order to develop its political role as a public service.

Reith's advocacy of a public service role for broadcasting in 1925 had the support of Post Office officials. Public opinion too had come round in favour of continuing broadcasting as a monopoly in the custody of the BBC, and there was no opposition to its transformation into a corporation at the end of the following year. Thereafter, for nearly thirty years, secure in its monopoly, the BBC was uniquely empowered to develop a service along the lines envisaged by its first Director-General.

There were two crucial decisions made by Reith and a handful of senior BBC staff about how to organize and deliver the programme service. The mandate of national service was interpreted most basically as meaning that anyone living anywhere in the United Kingdom was entitled to good quality reception of the BBC's programmes. They should be universally available to all. To achieve this a small number of twin transmitters were set up in strategically chosen locations to deliver two programmes to listeners: a regional programme produced from a handful of provincial centres, and a national programme produced from London. Wherever they lived listeners had the choice either of the national or their own regional programme. Second, the policy of mixed programming offered listeners on either channel a wide and varied range of programmes over the course of each day and week. Typically it included news, drama, sport, religion, music (light to classical), variety, and light entertainment. Not only did this mix cater for different needs (education, information, entertainment), but for different sectional interests within the listening public (children, women, farmers, businessmen, and so on).

These decisions had farreaching consequences. In the first place they brought into being a radically new kind of public – one commensurate with the whole of society. On behalf of this public the broadcasters asserted a right of access to a wide range of political, cultural, sporting, religious, ceremonial, and entertainment resources which, perforce, had hitherto been accessible only to small, self-selecting, and more or less privileged publics. Particular publics were replaced by the *general* public constituted in and by the general nature of the mixed programme service and its general, unrestricted availability. The fundamentally democratic thrust of broadcasting – of which Reith was well aware – lay in the new kind of access to virtually the whole spectrum of public life that radio made available to everyone. It equalized public life through the common access it established for all members of society – and it is worth noting that initially in nearly every case the broadcasters had a hard fight to assert that right on behalf of their audiences. In one particular case – the access of TV cameras to the House of Commons – the principle has only just been won.

In the long run these structural arrangements for the distribution of the service and the range of programmes on offer were far more important than the actual style and content of particular programmes at the time. The BBC soon succeeded in winning a reputation for itself as a purveyor of moral and cultural 'uplift' in the well established tradition of improvement for the masses. It was far less successful in establishing its news and political programmes. The monopoly, a source of strength in some areas of programming such as music, was a source of weakness in relation to parties, governments, and state departments. Throughout the era of its monopoly the BBC's independence of government was frail and it was widely regarded (especially overseas) as government's semi-official mouthpiece.

In the decade after the Second World War the monopoly came under increasing pressure, and the first postwar committee of inquiry into broadcasting – the 1950 Beveridge Committee – made the question of the monopoly its central concern. The BBC produced a classic defence of its position in its written submission to the committee. To introduce competition for audiences into broadcasting by establishing other programme services would inevitably lead to a lowering of programme standards. By that the BBC meant 'the purpose, taste, cultural aims, range and general sense of responsibility of the broadcasting service as a whole'.

> Under any system of competitive broadcasting all these things would be at the mercy of Gresham's Law. For, at the present stage of the nation's educational progress, it operates as remorselessly in broadcasting as ever it did in currency. The good, in the long run, will inevitably be driven out by the bad. It is inevitable that any national educational pyramid shall have a base immeasurably broader than its upper levels. The truth of this can be seen by comparing those national newspapers which have circulations of over four millions with those whose circulations are counted in hundred-thousands. And because competition in broadcasting must in the long run descend to a fight for the greatest number of listeners, it would be the lower forms of mass ·appetite which would more and more be catered for in programmes. (Beveridge 1950: para. 163)

In the event, the Beveridge Committee endorsed the BBC's monopoly, but its days were numbered. Within a couple of years a general election returned a Conservative government that rejected the recommendations of Beveridge and opted to establish commercial television, funded by advertising, in competition with the BBC's television service.

The British system is sometimes presented as a mixture of public service and commercial broadcasting as represented respectively by the BBC and ITV, but this is misleading. The terms under which commercial broadcasting was established by government made it part of the public service system from the beginning. A public corporation, the Independent Television Authority, was created by Act of Parliament with general responsibilities to establish a commercial television service that would inform, educate, and entertain. This service, known as Independent Television (ITV), was subject to state regulation and control by an authority charged with maintaining high standards of programme quality. It was an extension of public service broadcasting, not an alternative.

Even so, when the next committee on broadcasting, chaired by Sir Harry Pilkington, set about examining the impact of commercial television in 1960 and comparing its programme service with that of the BBC it found much to complain of in the doings of ITV. If the main concern of Beveridge had been with the monopoly, Pilkington was concerned with programme standards and the ominous threat of 'triviality'. Pilkington defined the concept of public service broadcasting as always to provide 'a service comprehensive in character; the duty of the public corporations has been, and remains, to bring to public awareness the whole range of worthwhile, significant activity and experience' (Pilkington 1960: 9). Against this criterion the committee noted the widespread public anxiety about television which had, in the last few years, taken over from radio as the dominant broadcasting medium. The commonest objection was that television programmes were too often designed to get the largest possible audience, and that to achieve this they appealed to a low level of public taste (Gresham's Law again). There was a lack of variety and originality, an adherence to what was safe, and an unwillingness to try challenging, demanding, and, still more, uncomfortable subject matter.

The committee had no hesitation in identifying commercial television as the culprit. The BBC was praised for its responsible attitude to the power of the medium of television. In the review of the BBC's performance there was a short paragraph on triviality – 'The BBC are aware of the liability of TV to fall into triviality, but have not always been successful in preventing this happening' (Pilkington 1960: 42) – but a whole page and a half were devoted to the problem of triviality in commercial television. The ITA was scolded for equating quality with box-office success, and was scathingly condemned for its inability to 'understand the nature of quality or of triviality, nor the need to maintain one and counter the other' (Pilkington 1960: 65). In short, commercial television was regarded as failing to live up to its responsibilities as a public service. It was not fit, in its present form, to extend its activities, and the plum that the committee had on offer – a third television channel – was unhesitatingly awarded to the BBC.

By the mid-1970s the terms in which the role of broadcasting in society was discussed had changed again, and the representations made to the committee on the future of broadcasting chaired by Lord Annan raised issues that would have seemed astonishing fifteen years earlier. The

Annan Report, published in 1977, noted a marked shift in the social, political, and cultural climate in Britain since the deliberations of its predecessor.

> For years British broadcasting had been able successfully to create, without alienating Government or the public, interesting and exciting popular network programmes from the world of reality as well as the world of fantasy – programmes on the arts and sciences, international reportage, political controversy, social enquiry, local investigation. These now began to stir up resentment and hostility, and protests against their political and social overtones.
>
> Hitherto it had been assumed – apart from the occasional flurry over a programme – that Britain had 'solved' the problem of the political relations of broadcasting to Government, Parliament and the public. Now people of all political persuasions began to object that many programmes were biased or obnoxious. But some, with equal fervour, maintained that broadcasters were not challenging enough and were cowed by Government and vested interests to produce programmes which bolstered up the *status quo* and concealed how a better society could evolve. (Annan 1977: 15)

Pilkington had praised the BBC and blamed ITV. Annan found both wanting – and the BBC rather more than ITV. The old monopoly had given way to a cosy 'duopoly' between the BBC and ITV who had both come to terms with competition by providing a broadly similar programme service with a roughly equal share of the audience. A significant spectrum of opinion, both among politicians and among the general public, was now calling a plague on both broadcasting houses. Broadcasting had become 'an overmighty subject' answerable neither to its political masters nor the general public. It was no longer representative of the increasingly diverse tastes, interests, and needs of an increasingly diverse society. Perhaps the only way to deal with the problem was to break up the existing broadcasting institutions.

The committee's response to the barrage of conflicting opinion it encountered was to opt for 'pluralism' – 'Pluralism has been the *leitmotiv* of all of us in this Report' it noted (Annan 1977: 108). It wanted to create a wider range of programmes that spoke not to the mass audience addressed by the existing duopoly but to those minorities and social groups whose needs and interests were not adequately served under the existing arrangments. It therefore recommended that the available fourth television channel should go to neither of the existing authorities but should be given to an independent Open Broadcasting Authority charged with the responsibility to develop a service that catered for all those interests presently underrepresented or excluded in the output of the BBC and ITV. The new authority would not produce any of its own programmes but, like a publishing house, would commission its programmes from a wide range of sources, including independent programme makers. The essential basis of what, in 1980, became Channel 4 was contained in Annan's concept of the Open Broadcasting Authority.

If hitherto public service broadcasting had been widely accepted in a largely unquestioning way, from Annan onwards old certainties crumbled. The defence of the original monopoly had been linked to a claim to a unified policy for programming that rested on a presumed social, cultural, and political consensus whose values were widely shared. But when that consensus collapsed what case could there be for a monopoly or a duopoly, or even the modest pluralism advocated by Annan? In the last decade there have been striking technological developments in broadcasting and telecommunications which, coupled with a sharp change in the political climate, have undermined all the old arguments in favour of public service broadcasting.

Today the key topic in debates about broadcasting is deregulation. Should the state cease to control and regulate broadcasting, and let market forces shape its future development? State regulation, the argument goes, was necessary from the beginning through to the end of the 1970s because in that period the scarcity of suitable wavelengths for broadcasting necessitated the intervention of the state to regulate their allocation and use. In this country there are at present only four national television channels, regulated by two authorities, broadcasting to the whole population, but change is only just around the corner. As the Peacock Report puts it:

> We are now in an unusually rapid technological advance in broadcasting. People can buy video recorders and watch films whenever they choose. Cable networks are beginning to develop in various parts of the country. There is already some broadcasting by satellite and, although it is impossible to predict its future precisely, it seems certain that its effects will be very large. . . . There is no reason why a large – indeed an indefinitely large – number of channels should not be brought into use. In the case of cable television fibre optic

communication techniques allow for two way communication and make pay TV a live possibility. (Peacock 1986: 2)

What will soon be available, at a price it is argued, is multi-channel access to a wide range of different video services and television programmes supported either by advertising, or by a fixed monthly charge or on a pay as you view basis. Whatever the precise mix of ways in which these services are financed and paid for it will not be by the licence fee method which has always been the means of financing the BBC. In this context why should people go on paying for the BBC as they do at present? It will become, after all, only one service out of many. It was this question that the Peacock Committee was asked by the government to consider in 1985 and its report was published the following year.

Other committees had considered broadcasting in social, cultural, and political terms. Peacock, set up to consider alternatives to the licence fee as a means of financing the BBC, applied a stringent economic approach and in so doing completely shifted the grounds of discussion. For Peacock, broadcasting was a commodity – a marketable good like any other – provided for consumers, and the establishment of consumer sovereignty in broadcasting through a sophisticated market system was the aim of the report. It defined a satisfactory broadcasting market as offering 'full freedom of entry for programme makers, a transmission system capable of carrying an indefinitely large number of programmes, facilities for pay-per-programme or pay-per-channel and differentiated charges for units of time' (Peacock 1986: 134). Consumer sovereignty meant the greatest freedom of choice for individuals via the widest provision of alternative broadcast goods. Neither the state nor delegated broadcasting authorities should continue to determine the nature and scope of the available broadcasting services. In future consumers should be the best judges of their own welfare.

Peacock envisaged a three-stage transition to a free market in broadcasting. In the crucial second stage (some time in the 1990s) it recommended that the BBC should be financed by subscription. Eventually, in the next century, a full market for broadcasting, with a very wide range of services via geo-stationary satellites and fibre-optic cable systems as well as traditional terrestrial broadcast services, would be based wholly on direct payment either for particular channels or programmes.

The committee recognized that these proposals might well lead to the erosion of public service broadcasting, and it was concerned to identify how the essential elements of public service broadcasting – which it defined as the production of a wide range of high quality programmes – might be retained. It wanted to protect those programmes of merit which, it acknowledged, would not survive in a market where audience ratings were the sole concern. To this end it suggested – though only in general terms – the establishment of a Public Service Broadcasting Council to secure the funding of public service programmes on any channel from stage two onwards. In spite of this gesture the whole tenor of the Peacock Report reversed the thinking of all previous parliamentary committees on broadcasting. Hitherto commercial considerations had taken second place to a public service commitment. Peacock, however, placed public service a long way second to commercial considerations and consumer choice. Public service broadcasting would no longer be the definitive feature of the British system.

Raymond Williams has identified the idea of *service* as one of the great achievements of the Victorian middle class, and one that deeply influenced later generations (Williams 1961: 313–17). It was certainly a crucial component of the ideal of public service as grafted onto broadcasting in its formative period from the 1920s to the 1950s. The Victorian reforming ideal of service was animated by a sense of moral purpose and of social duty on behalf of the community, aimed particularly at those most in need of reform – the lower classes. It was institutionalized in the bureaucratic practices of the newly emerging professional classes – especially in the reformed civil service of the late nineteenth century whose members saw themselves as public servants. At its best this passion for improving the lot of those below was part of a genuinely humane concern to alleviate the harsh consequences of a newly industrialized society. But it did nothing to change the balance of power in society, and maintained the dominance of the middle classes over the lower ranks.

One strand in this general concern for the conditions of the poor focused on their educational and cultural needs. A key figure in this development was Matthew Arnold (an inspector of schools for most of his working life) who believed that everyone was entitled to the enjoyment of those cultural treasures which, in his day, were available only to the educated classes. Arnold defined culture as 'the best that has been thought and written in the world' (quoted in Williams 1961: 124), a definition echoed by Reith in his advocacy of public service broadcasting. The radical element in Arnold's thinking was this claim that the state should use its authority to establish a fully national education system with a curriculum that included the study of the arts and humanities. Culture, for Arnold, was a means of alleviating the strain and hostility between classes in a deeply divided society, and the task of 'civilizing' the masses had a prudent political basis. It was a means of incorporating the working classes within the existing social and political order, and thus preventing the threat of revolt from below. Arnold's best known essay, *Culture and Anarchy*, expressed that fear in its very title.

The idea that the state should intervene in the terrain of culture and education, so daring in Arnold's time, had won a much wider acceptance some fifty years later at the time that broadcasting was established. Indeed, government intervention to control and regulate broadcasting and to define its general purposes is an early and classic instance of state intervention to regulate the field of culture. Victorian ideals of service laced with Arnoldian notions of culture suffused all aspects of the BBC's programme service in the thirty years of its monopoly. Such attitudes, in broadcasting as elsewhere, did not outlast the 1950s – or at least not with the degree of unself-critical certainty that they had hitherto possessed. 'The ideals of middle class culture', as the Annan Report put it, 'so felicitously expressed by Matthew Arnold a century ago. . . found it ever more difficult to accommodate the new expressions of life in the sixties' (Annan 1977: 14). Even so, it noted that at some levels the 'old Arnoldian belief in spreading "sweetness and light" still inspired the BBC' (Annan 1977: 80).

Underlying Arnoldian ideals of sweetness and light was a concern for social unity mingled with national pride. In the epoch of the BBC's monopoly both concerns were central to its role as a public service in *the national interest*. The linking of culture with nationalism – the idea of a national culture – was given new expression in broadcasting through those kinds of programme that had the effect of, in Reith's words, 'making the nation as one man'. From the 1920s through to today the BBC has continued this work of promoting national unity through such programmes. Sir Michael Swann, chairman of the BBC's Board of Governors, told the Annan Committee that 'an enormous amount of the BBC's work was in fact social cement of one sort or another. Royal occasions, religious services, sports coverage, and police series, all reinforced the sense of belonging to our country, being involved in its celebrations, and accepting what it stands for' (Annan 1977: 263). The report described the BBC as 'arguably the most important single cultural institution in the nation', and recommended preserving it as 'the natural interpreter of [great national occasions] to the nation as a whole' (Annan 1977: 79, 114).

Such occasions – exemplified by, say, the wedding of Prince Charles and Lady Diana Spencer – may indeed be moments of national unity in which all sections of society participate. But what of moments of crisis? The question then arises as to whose interests, in the last resort, broadcasting is there to serve – those of the state or the people? Governments claim the right to define the national interest and expect the broadcasters, particularly in a crisis, to uphold their definition of it. To defend the public interest may mean challenging the government of the day – a risky thing for institutions who derive their authority to broadcast from the government.

This politicized concept of the public interest has a very different history to that of public service, for the former relates to the news function of modern media and was elaborated in struggles for press freedom from the late eighteenth to the mid-nineteenth century. Against the power of the state, radical publics – bourgeois and proletarian – emerged to claim universal political and civil rights; the right to vote, to free speech and free assembly. A new kind of 'public sphere' was formed, independent of church and state, claiming the right to criticize both and committed to the establishment of public life, grounded in rational discussion, in which all members of society might participate (for a discussion of this concept in relation to broadcasting see Garnham 1986). The struggle to establish an independent press, both as a source of information about the activities of the state and as a forum for the formation and expression of public opinion, was part of this process, and an important aspect of the long battle for a fully democratic representative system of government.

The establishment of broadcasting coincided with the moment that the vote was finally conceded to all adult men and women, and the development of mass democracy is closely connected with broadcasting's role in that process. Reith was well aware of the importance of radio as a new organ of public opinion and as an instrument of democratic enlightenment, and was keen to move it in those directions. If the BBC was slow to develop a robust independence from the state it was not, as some have argued, the fault of its first Director-General. Nevertheless it is true to say that the political independence of broadcasting goes back no further than the mid-1950s. The introduction of strictly limited competition for audiences between the BBC and ITV gave the BBC something else to worry about other than its political masters. Competition in the sphere of news and current affairs had the effect of detaching the BBC from the apron strings of the state. Deference to political authority was replaced by a more populist, democratic stance as the broadcasters asserted the public's right to know by making politicians answerable and accountable to the electorate for their conduct of the nation's affairs. In news interviews, studio discussions and debates, current affairs magazine programmes, documentaries, and documentary dramas a whole clutch of political and social issues came onto the agenda through the medium of television – became part of the public domain, matters of common knowledge and concern. In this way broadcasting came to fulfil – never without difficulty, always under pressure – its role as an independent 'public sphere' and a forum for open public discussion of matters of general concern.

The extent of 'openness' is, however, something that varies according to the social, economic, and political climate. The thresholds of tolerance are not fixed. It is arguable, for instance, that television was more 'open' in the mid-1960s than the late 1970s. It is notable, however, that a Conservative government enhanced the 'public sphere' role of broadcasting at the beginning of the 1980s by authorizing Channel 4 to give special attention to the interests of minority groups and to commission a significant amount of its programmes from independent programme makers. The establishment of Channel 4 must be seen as the expression of a continuing political commitment to regulating broadcasting as a public good and in the public interest.

The pursuit of these aims has to date been underpinned by a disregard for commercial considerations as either the only or the primary objective of the broadcast services. This has manifested itself in two ways that are crucial to the realization of public service objectives: a policy of mixed programming on national channels available to all. Where commercial motives are primary broadcasters will go only for the most profitable markets – which lie in densely populated urban areas that can deliver large audiences without difficulty. The markets for cabled services are likely to prove even more selective: the affluent districts of major towns and cities will be wired up, while the poorer areas will be neglected. More sparsely populated, remoter areas will be ignored entirely. The long-term commitment of the BBC and IBA to make their services available to all has meant an investment out of all proportion to the returns in order to reach those regions that strictly economic considerations would simply neglect. The BBC set up sixty-five new transmitting stations in order to extend its service from 99 per cent of the population to the 99.1 per cent it reaches at present.

The alternative to mixed programming is generic programming – a channel that provides a service in which all or most of the programmes are of the same kind. Typically this has – on radio – meant particular kinds of music channel: classical, top forty, country and western, reggae or whatever. More recently, in the United States, generic TV channels have been established in cable services – Home Box Office (mainly movies), MTV (music videos), CNN (Cable News Network), as well as pay-per-view channels that offer mainly sporting fixtures. Generic programming fragments the general viewing public as still constituted, for instance, in the mixed programme service offered on the four national UK television channels. In so doing it destroys the principle of equality of access for all to entertainment and informational and cultural resources in a common public domain. Tht hard-won 'public sphere' created over the last thirty years on national television may shatter into splinters under the impact of deregulated multi-channel video services.

The Peacock Report has redefined broadcasting as a private commodity rather than a public good. Individual consumers, in the media universe of the next century as envisaged by Peacock, will choose what they want and pay for what they get. But consumers are not all equal in their purchasing power. The privatization of informational and cultural resources may well create a two-tiered society of those who are rich and poor in such resources. Such a development would undercut the fundamentally democratic principles upon which public service broadcasting rests.

In the political climate of today, public service broadcasting may seem a concept that has outlived its relevance. I do not think so. The history of its development in Britain has undoubtedly been coloured by the patrician values of a middle-class intelligentsia, and a defence of public service broadcasting in terms of quality and standards tied to prescriptive and elitist conceptions of education and culture is no longer feasible. But that has proved to be a contingent historical feature in the development of the BBC. Far more crucial has been the political will, until very recently, to maintain, against the grain of economic considerations, a commitment to properly public, social values and concerns in the system as a whole, that is, in the services provided by both the BBC and IBA. In my view equal access for all to a wide and varied range of common informational, entertainment, and cultural programmes carried on channels that can be received throughout the country must be thought of as an important citizenship right in mass democratic societies. It is a crucial means, perhaps the only means at present, whereby a common culture, common knowledge, and a shared public life are maintained as a social good equally available to the whole population. That was the basis of public service broadcasting as envisaged by John Reith, the much misunderstood first Director-General of the BBC. It is the basis of the present system. It should continue to be so in the future.

# References

Annan Committee, *Report of the Committee on the Future of Broadcasting* (Annan Report), Cmnd. 6753, London: HMSO, 1977.

Beveridge Committee, *Report of the Broadcasting Committee* (Beveridge Report), Cmnd. 8116, London: HMSO, 1951.

Crawford Committee, *Report of the Broadcasting Committee* (Crawford Report), Cmnd. 2599, London: HMSO, 1925.

Garnham, N., 'The media and the public sphere', in P. Golding, G. Murdock, and P. Schlesinger (eds), *Communicating Politics*, Leicester: Leicester University Press, 1986.

Peacock Committee, *Report of the Committee on Financing the BBC* (Peacock Report), Cmnd. 9284, London: HMSO, 1986.

Pilkington Committee, *Report of the Broadcasting Committee* (Pilkington Report), Cmnd. 1753, London: HMSO, 1960.

Reith, J., *Memorandum of Information on the Scope and Conduct of the Broadcasting Service*, Caversham, Reading: BBC Written Archive, 1925.

Sykes Committee, *Broadcasting Committee Report* (Sykes Report), Cmnd. 1951, London: HMSO, 1923.

Williams, R., *Culture and Society*, Harmondsworth: Penguin, 1961.

# Further reading

Home Office, *Broadcasting in the '90s: Competition, Choice and Quality*. London: HMSO, 1988.

MacCabe, Colin and Stewart, Olivia (eds), *The BBC and Public Service Broadcasting*, Manchester: Manchester University Press, 1986.

Peacock Committee, *The Report of the Broadcasting Committee*, Cmnd. 8116, London: HMSO, 1986, especially chapter 12.

Scannell, Paddy and Cardiff, David, *Serving the Nation: Public Service Broadcasting Before the War*, Milton Keynes: Open University Press, 1982.

For a fuller discussion of the wider implications of this chapter, see Paddy Scannell, 'Public service broadcasting and modern public life', *Media, Culture and Society*, vol. 11, no. 2 (April 1989).

# Postscript
*Andrew Goodwin and Garry Whannel*

Since this chapter was written the government White Paper *Broadcasting in the '90s* has been published. Among its main recommendations are:

● The present ITV system to be replaced by a regionally based third channel, which would have to include quality news and current affairs.

- The IBA and the Cable Authority to be replaced by a new Independent Television Commission, which would provide 'lighter touch' regulation.
- Channel 4's remit to be preserved but its advertising sold separately from ITV.
- The establishment of a fifth channel, starting in 1993, to be followed by a sixth if technically feasible.
- Franchises for Channel 3 and Channel 5 will run for 10 years and will be auctioned to the highest bidder.
- The BBC will be encouraged to progress towards the introduction of subscription-based services.

As this book goes to press there is clearly still much to be decided. Three things are already clear. The preservation of Channel 4's remit is a significant victory for public service broadcasting, but the changes in the conditions by which it receives revenue could be a crucial blow that will make following the remit very difficult. The new ITV system will inevitably be far more concerned with costs and far less concerned with programme quality. The BBC comes out relatively well – there has been no move as yet to dismantle its structure by statute, only a nudge, not a hefty shove.

Indeed one likely result of the expansion of broadcasting due to satellite and the reorganization of ITV will be the short-term strengthening of the BBC. The BBC currently makes fairly expensive programmes that for the most part are watched by large audiences. The cost per hour of the new satellite channels is much lower, and they could end up locked in a struggle with the new ITV companies for half of the audience, while the BBC remains fairly secure with its own 50 per cent.

But the more long-term outlook may be grimmer. In order to create the conditions for satellite and other new channels to thrive it may eventually be necessary to attack the present structure of the BBC. In particular the licence fee might be abolished to force the BBC to adopt a subscription system.

The underlying basis for current broadcasting policy stems, of course, from the shift, evident in the Peacock Report, away from a consideration of broadcasting as a social and cultural service for the community to broadcasting as the production of commodities, with viewers seen as consumers making choices in the market place.

There is little evidence so far that more will mean better. Everything suggests that the cost per hour of broadcasting as a whole will inevitably decrease considerably. Underlying the policy initiative is a desire to weaken the power of the broadcasting unions and increase casualization, both of which help to reduce the unit costs of independent production.

While it would be naive to adopt a simple cost = quality formula, there can be little doubt that the two have a close relation. Quality television can be made for £100,000 per hour or £25,000 per hour, and one can also spend £100,000 and make rubbish. However, it is very hard to make television of any quality at an average cost of less than £10,000 per hour. The irony of this new economistic approach to broadcasting is that by supposedly opening up the market to free consumer choice, it will precisely destroy the ability of the broadcasting industry to offer the range of choice currently available.

# 2 A SUITABLE SCHEDULE FOR THE FAMILY

*Richard Paterson*

The importance of television scheduling for the success of a channel has received increased recognition in recent years because of the BBC's achievements in regaining a dominant position in the competition for audiences against ITV. Some of this success is attributed to the 'art' of the scheduler. Exploiting the weaknesses of the opposition schedule by using strong programmes in particular time slots and deploying less popular material in less exposed positions are obvious strategies, but there are many other factors which must be considered.

In Britain the degree of change in a schedule from year to year tends to be quite restricted, dependent more upon new versions of old genres than on innovation in programme ideas. The uniqueness of the exceptional circumstances at the BBC in the mid-1980s, with its audience share set firmly on a downward path, did allow a renovation of the BBC schedule. However, this renovation was dependent on commissioned programmes: scheduling and commissioning are the related 'arts' necessary for success. What must be emphasized, then, is that the norm for a schedule is a set of fixed, virtually immutable points – and that continuities are as important as changes, except at times of crisis, as a history of scheduling shows. A process of change has occurred over the years, responding both to different perceptions of suitable programming by the programme makers and, as important, to the changing institutional context, particularly with regard to economic and social-moral forces.

In America, unbridled competition between the major networks has produced so called 'jugular' scheduling in which each network seeks to win as large an audience as possible. In Britain such competition has, until now, been circumscribed in a number of ways. First, our concept of public service broadcasting, requiring the broadcasters to educate, inform, and entertain, results in a commitment to a mixture of programme forms with – in the case of ITV – a range of mandatory requirements imposed on the schedule. Second, the diverse range of sources of finance modifies competition. ITV, funded by advertising revenue, needs to try and maximize audiences for its most popular programmes. BBC, funded by annual licence fees, is more concerned with maintaining an average audience share of at least 45 per cent. Channel 4 has been funded by an annual payment from the ITV companies, who in turn have had the right to sell advertising on the channel. Consequently Channel 4 has not been in direct competition with ITV, and with its statutory requirement to be innovatory it is currently surviving well on 5–10 per cent of the available TV audience. Third, there have been a series of informal agreements between BBC and ITV, such as the alternation of football coverage.

At its most basic, a schedule is the ordering of programmes across a day, week by week. It forms a framework with which the viewer becomes familiar, so that s/he returns to watch a programme at a known time every week. One factor for the scheduler is the matching of the available audience at different times of day to programme provision – constructing the audience, or responding to its needs, depending on your point of view.

### The scheduler's lexicon

*Channel loyalty*: It used to be felt that many viewers tend to watch one channel predominantly, would turn to it automatically, and then tend to stay with it. Consequently great emphasis was laid on the need to win viewers at the start of an evening. The expansion in the range of choice with the introduction of BBC 2 in 1964 and Channel 4 in 1982, and the spread of domestic video in the 1980s, are all felt to have eroded channel loyalty.

*Inheritance factor*: If a programme gets a large audience the following programme can reasonably expect to inherit a proportion of that audience. The 8 p.m. slot following *Coronation Street* has often been used to introduce new programmes to the audience.

*Pre-echo*: People will often tune in early to watch a favourite programme. They will often see the last few minutes of the preceding programme, and may then decide to watch all of it the following week.

*Hammocking*: A less popular programme can be hammocked by placing it between two popular ones, so that it benefits from inheritance at the start and pre-echo towards the end. For many years *World in Action* was placed after an 8 p.m. sitcom and before a crime series such as *The Sweeney*.

*Common junction points*: Where two programmes start at the same time on BBC 1 and BBC 2, or on ITV and Channel 4, the opportunity is available for cross-trailing. BBC make use of this, with the familiar phrase, 'And now a choice of viewing on BBC. . .'.

*Demographics*: A term used in the advertising industry for describing the composition of the audience in age, class, and gender terms.

*Target audiences*: Can be used by television producers to describe the audience a programme is aimed at or by the advertising industry to describe the audience that a particular product is aimed at. The aim of advertising agencies is to find programmes whose audience profile matches their own target audience, although ultimately the cost of particular advertising slots is usually the overriding consideration.

These terms have largely been inherited from American television. However, even in the British context, the practices which they indicate can to a limited extent be seen to operate and to affect programme placement. But the high percentage of homes with domestic video and second sets has eroded the power of schedulers to determine our range of choice, and the prospect of further change is great, with the launch of satellite channels, available to all viewers with small satellite dishes.

A major problem for schedulers is how to place a programe which is perceived to have little attraction for a mass audience. The response varies across the different channels. The minority channels (BBC2 and Channel 4) to a certain extent concede much of prime time to their larger partners and fulfil their remit to be 'different' in these slots. The two main channels also carry some 'minority' programming (usually current affairs and documentary) in prime time – for the BBC an inheritance of the Reithian notion of stretching the audience, for ITV an imposition by the IBA. Such programmes, as well as any which are not guaranteed success, are hammocked between stronger programmes, in the expectation that they will inherit much of the audience which watches the programme preceding it, and may want to stay to watch the programme that follows it. With the growth of cross-trailing at common junction .points, the power of the inheritance factor has been somewhat diminished.

32

Television institutions invariably consider their key task to be that of satisfying, in some way, the needs of an audience. Viewers are seldom thought of as a homogenous mass, but more as an overlapping series of groups with various interests. In the current duopolistic system, competition has been tempered by other obligations and these include, for the commercial system regulated by the IBA, a family viewing policy (in existence since the early 1960s); mandated network programmes at specified times (*The News*, current affairs, *The South Bank Show*,); and restrictions on the amount of certain types of programmes, such as game shows. The value of game show prizes is also limited by the IBA.

The limited-term contracts also allow the IBA informally to impose conditions which the contractors have sought to meet in order to ensure renewal. This led to the production of culturally prestigious and expensive programmes, although often (as with *Brideshead Revisited*) shrewd groundwork was done on promoting overseas sales. But the changes in the company structure and programme policies of LWT at the start of the 1970s and of TV-AM in the early 1980s demonstrated that the power of the IBA could be limited in practice.

However, a central notion in any understanding of the structures of television programming, in its aesthetic, economic, or cultural modes, is that it is addressed to viewers in the home. It is a domestic medium and the space of domestic life, the family household, invokes a set of understandings which inform scheduling and consequently the commissioning of programmes.

A family viewing policy is in operation on all four British channels, under which particular sorts of programme or scenes portraying violence and sexuality cannot be screened before 9 p.m., when children are assumed to be watching in greater numbers, possibly without adult supervision. The policy is rooted in normative assumptions about the family. In the early evening, domestic life is assumed to be devoted to meals and the audience is understood to be unable to concentrate for long spells. Television is in the control of the child audience with parents available intermittently until about 7.30 p.m. From this time the mother is thought to control the television, which functions for the next 90 minutes as a focus of the family. After 9 p.m., when the rules on content are less strict, children's viewing is seen as the responsibility of the parent. Control of the television set is shared between the adults with the father assumed to take a much more central role in determining programme choice.

Clearly such circumstances apply to only a minority of homes and it has often been pointed out that less than one-third of all households contain a family with children (see, for example, *Family Expenditure Survey*, London: HMSO, 1984). However, such is the power of commonsense discourses, backed by research, that these models of the audience have a big influence on programme planning. The understood patterns of domestic life (with, for ITV companies, regional variations to consider) helps to determine the structure of programmes commissioned for particular slots. For example, early evening programmes, from *Tonight* through *Crossroads* to *Wogan*, are characteristically fragmented and episodic, and can be followed without demanding complete and continuous attention from an audience.

It should be noted, too, that the importance of television in the economic domain is a factor in overdetermining this structure. Television in Britain, certainly since the mid-1950s, has become, as in many other societies, an instrument of modernization and consumerism. The demographic profile of an audience is all-important to an advertising-supported channel which sells audiences to advertisers, and gets those audiences according to its success in programming.

Audience measurement, by Broadcasters' Audience Research Bureau, is produced each week from figures derived from meters in a representative sample of about 2,000, which record the time a set is switched on and off, and the channel it is tuned to. The figures are broken down into class, age, gender, and regional groups. Generally the most popular programmes are also those most popular with each individual group and traditionally television advertisers have tended to be more interested in the sheer size of an audience rather than its composition. However some programmes do have skewed audiences in terms of class, age, or gender, and these allow the advertising agency buyers to spread their advertising spots across the schedule to pick up sufficient members of any particular target group. The problem for ITV has been that its schedule appeals to an audience skewed towards the older and lower-class groups in British society, not the groups of most interest to advertisers. The value of Channel 4 has been its ability to attract higher-class profiles for its audiences and an ability to retain younger audiences.

The target audiences have changed over the years. At one time it was housewives who were sought, and endless advertisements for household goods were delivered in programmes they were found to watch. The range of products advertised has changed over the years so that in 1986 and 1987 financial advertising, including that for corporations being privatized and for general corporate prestige, dominated advertising time for long periods of the year. It is not evident that this has had clear effects on the schedule, although coverage of financial matters has increased.

34

The fragmentation of audiences in the wake of the establishment of Channel 4 and the use of the video recorder both for time-shifting and for viewing hired tapes has slightly undermined the certainties of the 1970s and has introduced a more sophisticated notion of target audiences, but the main thrust of current scheduling remains that of attracting particular groups perceived to have spending power.

The BBC is not beset by the problem of audience profile quite as directly as the commercial system. Its schedule is freed of such pressures and is more able to experiment to a limited degree. However, the duopolistic system has inevitably created similarities between the services. For example, for many years BBC and ITV found it best to schedule their current affairs coverage at the same time. So *Panorama* and *World in Action* occupied the same slot, until Michael Grade moved *Panorama* to 9.25 p.m. with surprising success.

The key to television schedules is still repetition and continuity, and it is only over long periods, or occasionally in the short sharp example of popular 'innovation' (for instance with *The Singing Detective*), that changes in television's forms and its address to the nation can be discerned. There have undoubtedly been major changes in the mores of the nation in the past twenty years and this has been reflected in programming, but there is much unchanged. *Coronation Street* has been on air since 1960, *World in Action* since 1963, *Emmerdale Farm* since 1972, *The South Bank Show* since 1978, *News at Ten* since 1967.

Goodhardt, Ehrenberg, and Collins have shown that the audience for any one episode of a serial or series is not the same as for the next in its composition. Repeat viewing is more a function of social habits (i.e. people's availability) than of programme loyalty. Only 55% of the viewers of one episode of a series watch the following episode. However, television schedules depend upon audiences knowing where to find the programmes. One of the great difficulties for the single programme, not thematically connected to any series, is to get an audience to find it and sample it. Similar problems face broadcasting organizations when a new series is about to start.

In the USA series are often cancelled mid-season if they are failing to get a good enough rating. Such a fate seldom comes to British programmes – some (such as *Studio*) are moved to less damaging points in the schedule if they are faltering, and a failed soap opera (such as *Albion Market*) is quietly ditched.

The important role of the presentation departments of television in trailing new programmes has been little studied. Similarly the central role of coverage in newspapers and in programme journals has to be acknowledged in creating audiences, or at least in encouraging audiences to sample new programmes.

The continuity and promotion function between the programmes in a way that mirrors the practices of the scheduler in the quest for audiences, and practices vary across the industry. The key function of trailers is to maximize the audience for a channel's programmes. In the federal ITV system there are great differences in the practice of the companies; each have different priorities and interests in what to trail, reflecting amongst other things their view of the region's audience. This is a significant detail which tends to be forgotten when broad generalizations about the duopoly are being made, and has effects, too, on the basic ITV schedule which allows room for regional variation in many respects.

Cross-promotion of Channel 4 and ITV is now common; however, the two BBC channels only note what is on the other channel at programme junctions with little attempt to trail alternatives ahead of time. At the BBC, promotion, decided by the channel controller, usually features one programme or series quite heavily each week. One of the most significantly successful campaigns was that for *EastEnders* in 1985. It featured fifty-nine completely separate trailers before the serial went on air – each shown only once.

For the BBC, the space between programmes – trailers, presentation announcements, and station identity logo – is an important factor in carrying the image of the BBC's diverse programming and in ensuring a continuity of audience from one programme to the next. On ITV, in contrast, such material has to jostle for space and attention alongside advertising.

Both the BBC and ITV, then, use trailing first and foremost to create attention for new programming. Sometimes it may be used in an attempt to boost programmes which are under-performing; an interesting example was the attempt, ultimately not achieved, to keep alive *Albion Market*, the Granada twice-weekly serial which failed to gain an audience in its Friday/Sunday slots.

Clearly, the key question for the broadcasters is the placement of the trailers in the pre-existing schedule where viewers likely to sample the programme on offer might be found. The 'watershed' content rules of the family-viewing policy continue to operate for trailers, complicating trailer placement further. For most broadcasters the selection of spots seems to depend in the main on intuition, with notions of contiguity of interest and similarity of audience the main factors. In some organizations the broadcasters adopt a strategy similar to that of the advertising-space buyer, looking at ratings and demographics to maximize trailer impact.

One function of trailers is to fill out time, when a programme, particularly an 'American hour' series episode, underruns the slot time. American series run for 46 minutes, rather than the 52 minutes for British commercial programmes. IBA regulations allow a maximum of 7½ minutes of advertising for each hour, so the remainder has to be filled with presentations and trailers. One of the weapons used by the BBC in the attempt to regain its audience share was the aggressive undermining of these weak spots in the ITV schedule, so that programmes were started at their announced starting time to draw in audiences who were offered endless trailers as alternative viewing.

One result of the continuing sequence of programmes, trailers, station identification, programme announcements, and, on commercial television, advertisements, is that the experience of watching television can be seen as one of consuming not discrete items but a continuous flow of material. Raymond Williams[1] analyses television precisely as a flow, characterized by a lack of explicit connection between elements, and organized around the values of speed, variety and miscellany.

The greater the competition for viewers in order to increase revenue directly the more marked the flow character of television becomes. This is because the flow helps to disguise the breaks in programmes and mask potential channel-switching moments.[2]

In fact, on close analysis it makes more sense to understand television not so much as a flow but rather as sets of relatively short segments, often grouped within programmes.[3] Indeed some argue that, with greater access to video, with its facility to play, freeze, speed up, and slow down, the growth in channels, and the increased tendency to zap between channels, the viewer now has an ability to recompose television. Evidence about this form of viewer behaviour is still sparse, however, and the power of the scheduler is still a major element in the system of television.

Complementary to on-air trailers are the promotion of programmes through the *Radio Times* and *TV Times*, and equally important, although out of the direct control of the broadcasters, daily and weekly newspaper coverage. Each programme journal is promoted on-air each week and there is close liaison with the ITV companies and the BBC channel controllers on the choice of front cover image.

The importance of the *TV Times* and *Radio Times* can be gauged from their circulation figures and by the high price for display advertising in each journal. Interestingly they are important vehicles for advertisers to address the family audience so central to the whole ideology of television programming. Each enters homes across the nation and is read by a diverse audience from all classes, ages, and groups who use it to map their television watching on to their own lived schedule. Both programme journals thus have an important relationship to the architecture of the schedule – on the one hand mapping it for the potential viewer, on the other promoting particular programmes.

The central feature of all these elements is the perception that it is the family audience which is being addressed, first and foremost, although not exclusively. It is this notion which underpins and informs the construction of the schedule. In parallel with the television regime's working practice which defines repetition as a fundamental structuring principle of most of its programming – on the basis that viewers more easily watch that with which they are familiar – the schedule is determined by notions of family life.

Repetition inevitably has an inertial effect on the possibility of change and innovation. The set weekly pattern of programmes – *Coronation Street* invariably at 7.30 on Mondays, Wednesdays, and Fridays, *News at Ten* virtually unmovable on weekday evenings, for example – has a large number of virtues for the broadcaster, and for the viewer. It allows a predictability of resource deployment within television organizations, and it makes particular schedule points easy to remember for audiences. The series and serial have come to dominate television to such an extent that even the single documentary is now usually anthologized under an umbrella series title, be it *First Tuesday*, *Forty Minutes* or *Viewpoint*.

The key drawback to these practices is the increased difficulty faced by the one-off or quirky programme, which not only is hard to fit into the schedules, unless there is an overwhelming reason for its inclusion, but also necessitates a high degree of exposure and trailing, which will only pay off for a one-schedule slot. Hence, mini-series are preferable to one-off plays, and anthology titles begin to predominate; but the series or serial are the most cost-effective form.

The fact that it is the concept of family viewing which dominates the construction of the schedule has been little studied. Even the recent work of David Morley, Peter Collett, and Michael Svennevig tends towards a realist account of TV watching by families.[4] Peter Collett's research used video cameras hidden over a television to observe viewing behaviour.[5] This, and interviewing family members, offers interesting descriptions of actions, which are, however, not explained. An explanation of activity has to come to terms with the intentions of those organizing the time, as well as the various factors which affect both these actors and the changing formation of the family.

Of course the advertising industry has long valued a knowledge of family consumption behaviour, and broadcasters have deployed versions of a family viewing policy over many years, even back to the early days of radio broadcasting. In the concerted campaign to attain a family viewing policy in the late 1950s there were overlapping concerns to control what should be shown when: those worried about the damaging effect of certain television programmes, particularly on children (a consistent preoccupation in many quarters), allied with the advertising industry's desire for knowledge of, and a certain predictability about, the audience for their clients' products at different times of the day.

Every week the Broadcasters' Audience Research Bureau (BARB) carries out various types of audience research, particularly about audience size and composition. It classifies the population by region (because of the federal/regional nature of the ITV system) in the following demographic categories: Males and Females by age (0–15, 16–24, 25–34, 45–54, 55–64, and 65+) and by class (AB, C1, C2, D, and E). It also subclassifies men as working/not working, and women/housewives (not always synonymous categories) as 'working' or 'not working'.

This demographic breakdown allows advertisers to target particular audiences for specific products. The patterns of TV programming reinforce preconceived ideas of family life, and the placement of advertisements overlays these programmes, but also determines in a circular way what sorts of programme are commissioned for particular slots. Advertising-space buyers organize spots across the schedule to achieve a particular audience profile with clear effects inside the commercial TV companies. Each company maintains an advertising sales force and develops a 'marketing profile' of its region, with detailed breakdowns of consumption habits, lifestyle, retail outlets, and population, aimed to induce new clients to advertise.

The commercial channels are only half of the 1980s map of British broadcasting but their influence on the BBC has been crucial in determining the architecture of the schedule there, too. The introduction of the *Tonight* current affairs programme into the toddlers truce in 1957 – the period between 6.00 and 7.00 had previously had no TV programmes on the assumption that parents needed this time to put their children to bed – was determined by the competitive environment. So too was the extended use of daytime, and the BBC's decision to compete at breakfast time. This competitive environment is itself constrained by informal rules ·of public service standards, defined by an evolved web of practices which have responded to pressures from different quarters over the years.

The most fundamental changes in the broadcast schedule have occurred at times of flux. Many of the key dispositions were made soon after the introduction of commercial television during a period of fundamental reformulation of ground rules, political, social, and moral, in British society. Since then the fluidity of certain arrangements has to be attributed to the important interaction of broadcasting, the most important contemporary cultural medium, and the dominant political forces at any time. However, alongside fundamental changes there have been many continuities.

What is now in question is how far the rules of scheduling informed by family-viewing principles remain appropriate to new regimes of broadcasting, particularly now that multiple satellite-delivered channels are available to households. With the increasing number of multi-set households the audience can be fragmented at any time of day. This leads to a possible economic viability for thematic and minority channels and forces broadcasting provision further into the market. Scheduling for the family may well become a historical curiosity if satellite uptake is significant.

The Peacock Report in 1986 sought deregulation in broadcasting with the consumer deemed sovereign in his or her choice of programmes, for which payment would be made. The closing of the public service era of television will be determined by technological, political and economic considerations, and will be taking place at the same time as the reworking of social and political agendas. The notion of broadcasting as a public good, whereby each additional consumer adds nothing to production costs, and of public service as the key principle in programme provision for all segments of the population have been fundamentally questioned.

However, the contradictions of a desire to deregulate alongside a wish to ensure the reduction in violent and sexual content have yet to be worked through. What is certain is that conceptions of the family and family life will be invoked when any regulations are created. A quick glance at the campaign against the video nasties in the early 1980s shows the effectiveness and power of such concerns. A suitable schedule for the family will certainly be uppermost in the minds of the legislators as they tackle the multi-channel future.

## Notes

1 R. Williams, *Television: Technology and Cultural Form*, London: Fontana, 1974.
2 R. Altman, 'Television sound', in T. Modleski (ed.), *Studies in Entertainment: Critical Approaches to Mass Culture*, Bloomington and Indianapolis: Indiana University Press, 1986.
3 J. Ellis, *Visible Fictions*, London: Routledge & Kegan Paul, 1982.

4 D. Morley, *Family Television: Cultural Power and Domestic Leisure*, London: Comedia, 1986. See also D. Morley, *The 'Nationwide' Audience*, London: British Film Institute, 1980; M. Svennevig, 'The viewer viewed', paper to the Second International Television Studies Conference, July 1986, University of London; B. Gunter and M. Svennevig, *Behind and in Front of the Screen: Television's Involvement with Family Life*, London: Libbey, 1987.

5 P. Collett, 'Watching the TV audience', paper to the Second International Television Studies Conference, July 1986, University of London.

## Further reading

Goodhardt, G.J., Ehrenberg, A.S.C., and Collins, M.A., *The Television Audience: Patterns of Viewing*, Farnborough: Saxon House, 1975, 2nd edn 1987.

Gray, A., 'Behind closed doors: video recorders in the home', in Helen Baehr and Gillian Dyer (eds), *Boxed In: Women and Television*, London: Pandora, 1987.

Lull, J., *World Families Watch Television*; London: Sage, 1988.

Paterson, R., 'Planning the family; the "art" of scheduling', *Screen Education*, no. 35 (Summer 1980).

Pilsworth, M. 'An imperfect art – TV scheduling in Britain', *Sight and Sound*, vol. 49, no. 4 (Autumn 1980).

# 3 TV NEWS: STRIKING THE RIGHT BALANCE?

*Andrew Goodwin*

What the BBC and ITN present as news is not news at all: it is pure, unadulterated bias. (Arthur Scargill)

I would like to be able to read a newspaper or magazine, or watch the news on television, without having to make constant translations and adjustments for exaggerations and bias. (Princess Anne)

For most people in Britain, television news remains the most pervasive and most trusted source of information about the world. Television news is generally given greater credence by the public than either newspapers or radio; probably because it is perceived to be less partisan than the press, and because it offers the 'evidence' of pictures that isn't available on radio. News broadcasts are also some of television's most popular sources of programming: the evening news programmes from the BBC and ITN regularly feature in the high spots of the ratings. Unsurprisingly, discussion of television news has been controversial and contentious. Much of it has centred on accusations of 'bias', and that debate will be the subject of this chapter.

### From radiovision to Birtism

In the development of television news over the last forty years, three trends are clearly evident. First there has been a great expansion in the amount of news broadcast. Many new developments in British television have been built upon or around news programmes – breakfast television, the central role of ITN's *Channel 4 News* in the fourth channel's schedule, various proposals for all-news cable services like the USA's Cable News Network. Secondly, the presentation of news has become increasingly popular in its tone. A great deal of television news today is closer in style to the 'popular' press than the so-called 'quality' newspapers. Thirdly, news has become increasingly controversial, just like the events it represents. As the social and political consensus has broken down in postwar Britain, so television has encountered more and more problems in knowing how to represent that world. As a consequence, television news has found itself embroiled in numerous controversies about its handling of contentious stories: in the last ten years there have been major arguments about its coverage of Irish politics, the so-called 'winter of discontent' in 1979, the South Atlantic war of 1982, the 1984/5 miner's strike, the US bombing of Libya in 1985, and its coverage throughout this period of Mrs Thatcher's Conservative Party.

The early days of British television have been described, by Asa Briggs, as the 'era of Radiovision'.[1] Television was seen as a service that provided radio, but with pictures. And so it was with news, where this notion informed the production of news bulletins as late as the mid-1950s. In the prewar period (1936–9), the BBC agreed with MGM and Gaumont to screen two of their film newsreels each week. When that arrangement broke down after the war, the BBC began to produce its own newsreel, starting in January 1948. The history of television news is full of surprises, and the first of these occurred now: television news was not produced by the News Division of the BBC, but by its Film Department. Until 1954 the News Division output was restricted to a 10-minute bulletin – in sound only! The script was read over a caption. When the News Division was finally allowed to produce its own programmes, with pictures, it continued to flout one of the golden rules of journalism, the drive for an 'exclusive' – the BBC never had an 'exclusive' story because it would not run an item unless at least one news agency had confirmed it. Futhermore, although the new format (under the name *News and Newsreel*) employed pictures, its news values did not reflect the visual nature of the medium. The BBC's news at this time was gathered, selected, and presented using news values derived from radio – 'picture value' was not a consideration.

These strange tales are significant, for two reasons. First, they point to a lack of a journalistic tradition in the BBC, which to this day rarely 'breaks' a story. TV news has been marked by a consistent lack of interest in 'investigative' journalism. This is relevant to the discussion of 'bias', as we shall see, for one mechanism that might generate bias in television news is the tendency for television to respond to a news agenda established by the press.

Secondly, these remarks demonstrate a pervasive fear of the visual in British television. In news production this often meant that editors and producers were concerned that if picture value began to dictate news selection then more sophisticated (that is, literary) news values would suffer. The pioneering BBC producer Grace Wyndham Goldie puts it like this:

> If, in the opinion of an experienced news editor, a news story merited only twenty seconds, but there was some specially shot film of it which could not really make its point in less than half a minute, what should he do? Abandon news values and show the film even if this meant cutting the length of another and more important news story of which there was only meagre film illustration? But that would be an abandonment of BBC news standards.[2]

It is interesting to note that this comment from a television producer has found an echo among many critics of television, who are wont to bemoan the 'trivialization' involved in the predominance of visual imagery. The bestselling book *Amusing Ourselves to Death*, by US critic Neil Postman, makes exactly the same point — that television's picture values are inherently inferior to those of print.[3] It is also interesting to note that implicit in this fear of the visual is an acknowledgement that television is not in fact a 'window on the world', as is so often claimed by television professionals. News standards are derived from the broadcasters, not the world they seek to represent. And when television offers a photographic 'reflection' of it, the whole truth and nothing but the truth may not be the result.

Eventually the BBC's standards had to shift. The arrival of commercial television in 1955 led to the development of a very different kind of news broadcast. The commercial network set up a separate organization, Independent Television News (ITN), to produce a nightly bulletin very different in tone from the BBC's. It had 'newscasters' (a term derived from television in the USA), including Robin (now Sir Robin) Day, who recalls:

> As one of ITN's original newscasters, my job was to break with the BBC tradition of announcer-read national news. The ITN newscaster

44

was to use his own knowledge and personal style. He was also to be a reporter going out to gather news with the camera crews.[4]

ITN turned the news into a programme in its own right, adding entertainment values and developing the now familiar 'tailpiece' which wraps up each broadcast on a humorous or eccentric note. According to Day, ITN followed 'a middle road between the BBC and the popular press'.

The BBC maintained a more serious approach (it is impossible even now to imagine Reggie Bosanquet reading the BBC news), but made a number of concessions to the new style. It acquired personality newscasters and began to emulate ITN in both the selection and presentation of news. By the 1980s entertainment values had become so important for the popularity of news programmes that the BBC could lead off its main evening bulletin with an item about an incident concerning a fictional character – the shooting of J.R. on *Dallas*.

In the 1980s three related trends have taken root. First, it should be noted that the rise of Thatcherism in British politics left the old liberal values of public service broadcasting somewhat high and dry. As British politics moved significantly to the right the degree of 'fit' between the political values of politicians and broadcasters was disturbed. The result was a barrage of complaints from the Conservative Party and other rightwing organizations that broadcasting was too 'leftwing'.

A second trend is the associated deregulation of the media and the related decentralization of television news. This is occurring mainly outside the existing broadcast networks (for instance, in cable and satellite television), but broadcast television has also decentralized some of its news output – for instance, London Weekend Television's decision to 'buy in' a news service instead of producing it in-house.[5]

Thirdly, there is the phenomenon of 'Birtism'. In 1975 *The Times* ran a series of articles by television producer John Birt and presenter Peter Jay which argued that television news harboured a 'bias against understanding'. They complained that news was too superficial and made proposals designed to provide more analysis in the presentation of stories. John Birt went on to put his ideas into practice as producer of LWT's *Weekend World* – a 60-minute current affairs programme often entirely devoted to the analysis of one story. In 1987 Birt became Deputy Director-General at the BBC and began instituting some of his ideas. Whether this will redress the trend towards entertainment values in television news remains to be seen, but what it doesn't address is the abiding accusation of 'bias' levelled at the broadcasters.

## Getting the balance right

Because broadcasting was established as a monopoly (and thereafter as a duopoly) it was decided that, unlike the press, it should not be permitted to broadcast editorial opinion, as newspapers do in their 'editorial' pages (and, increasingly, in their news output also). From the very outset the broadcasters have been required to observe the strictures of impartiality. The Licence and Agreement which alongside the Royal Charter of 1926 established the BBC requires it to 'refrain from . . . expressing the opinion of the Corporation on current affairs or matters of public policy'. Those principles still apply today. And similar passages were written into the various Acts of Parliament that established commercial broadcasting, obliging it to 'observe due impartiality . . . as respects matters of political or industrial controversy or relating to current public policy'.

The broadcasters have often substituted the term 'balance' for 'objectivity'. This term wisely implies that while objectivity might not be possible, at least the range of possible interpretations is fairly represented. According to the strictures of balance, both or all sides of a conflict deserve a fair hearing in news coverage. Yet despite the ideology of balance, and the fact that television news seems to be so widely trusted, many critics have charged that 'bias' and not 'balance' is the word that most accurately describes it.

Charges of bias have emanated from a wide range of sources, as the quotes that head this chapter suggest. But by far the most comprehensive objections come from the Left and the trade union movement. The most ambitious and controversial criticism of television news have come from the Glasgow University Media Group, whose work now spans more than ten years of research and has been very influential in the British labour movement. In *Really Bad News*, members of the Glasgow Media Group state:

> Our conclusion was that television is biased to the extent that it violates its formal obligations to give a balanced account. Our research also led us to discover that the broadcast institutions are extremely hierarchical, that close links exist between them and a range of 'official' and 'accepted' sources. The result of this is that the news gives preferential treatment to some ways of seeing the world.

The Glasgow Group's best-known studies emerged from their first research project, which looked at television news on all channels in the first half of 1975. (This study was first written up in the book *Bad News* and is summarized, along with most of the group's work, in *Really Bad*

*News.*[6]) During this period they tested their hypothesis that television news systematically favoured socially dominant groups by investigating its coverage of a whole series of different stories, including the topic of inflation and its causes (a major story at that time). In this study they found that television news tended to offer one explanation for inflation (high wages) far more often than other competing explanations (rising prices, the energy crisis, economic recession, the nature of the capitalist economic system). The group found that during the first four months of 1975 there were 287 occasions when views supportive of the government's policy of wage restraint were aired, while opposing positions were broadcast only seventeen times.

These kinds of statistics are representative of many they cite, and give an insight into their method, which is generally that of conducting an analysis of news coverage of a particular theme and then comparing it to interpretations that have been offered outside the media. Invariably the group find that television's explanations draw from a narrow range of views that tend to favour the rich and the powerful. Importantly, the group do not suggest that these are random, occasional errors. They seek to show that television routinely engages in a form of tunnel vision that favours one area of the political spectrum and one side of industry.

It is no use, in the face of this, for broadcasters to object (as they sometimes have) that all reporting involves some degree of error. That is not in dispute. Of course it does not substantiate the bias argument to discover inaccuracies or mistakes in news coverage. It has to be shown that the errors are routine and – most importantly – that they systematically work to favour one side of the story.

The Glasgow Group claim to have discovered this. They argue that industrial coverage tends to emphasize disputes at the expense of many other kinds of stories, and systematically excludes the work trade unions undertake when they are not involved in strikes. Union activity is represented almost entirely in terms of strikes and is portrayed as irrational and unmotivated. Furthermore the language used by reporters and presenters is far from impartial. References to the 'car workers' strike' or the 'railman's dispute' imply that the workers are the cause of the strike, not management or the government. And whereas terms such as 'reject', 'demand', and 'threaten' are used when referring to unions and workers, the group note that more positive terms such as 'offer' or 'promise' are used where employers are concerned.

The Glasgow Group's criticisms do not stop there, however. They charge that the selection of interviewees on television reflects further bias, and in their study of a strike involving Glasgow dustcart workers in 1975 they note that not one striker was interviewed. The location of interviews is also important. When workers are shown on streets and picket lines, this gives them less credibility than managers and government spokespersons who are shown with all the authority of large desks and book-lined rooms. And while the broadcasters claim that the often hostile line and tone of questioning is simply a case of the interviewer playing 'Devil's advocate', the Glasgow Group give examples where a much softer line is adopted for employers and government representatives.

It is also central to their case that when opposing views are presented, in an effort to maintain balance, they rarely act to structure the overall framework of debate:

> Information which contradicts the dominant view, if it appears at all, exists as fragments and is never explored by news personnel as a rational alternative explanation. It is not used by them as a way of organising what they cover, or selecting what they film, or structuring their interviews.

In other words, oppositional views appear, but only within a framework set out by their opponents.

This is the phenomenon of 'agenda setting', where the media do not only distort the world that is represented, but help to structure public perception of it by *omission* as well as inclusion. The media might not tell us what to think, but perhaps they tell us what to think *about*. Certain questions are taken for granted in television coverage of news: it is assumed that 'we' all want what is best for 'Britain', that 'we' want the strike to end, that 'we' are opposed to 'extremism' and that 'moderation' is always desirable. Whether or not we do in fact agree with these assumptions, the point is that these beliefs are usually implied, and work to structure the whole framework of debate, regardless of examples of distortion in reporting. If it seems outrageous to suggest that television news omits questions such as the positive effects of strikes on worker solidarity and the possible advantages to be gained from 'damaging' Britain's economy (weakening British capitalism, for instance) that is merely evidence of how powerfully it *has* set the agenda for coverage of industrial disputes.

It is important to understand that the Glasgow Group are not proposing a conspiracy thesis, in which broadcasters and the powerful plot to brainwash the public. They regard much of this bias to be the result of the unconscious professional practices and class background of television journalists, editors, and producers. In an earlier draft of this chapter, I wrote the phrase 'the miner's strike' at one point, without

48

thinking of its implications, because (like many journalists) I am habituated to hearing such formulations. The 'bias' was far from deliberate or conscious . . . and it was not the result of a conspiracy!

## Another side of the story

Of the many critics of the Glasgow Media Group, the broadcasters themselves have been the most public and the least sophisticated. They have accused the group of political bias and cast doubt on their methods, but in such a defensive manner that anyone considering their response is bound to conclude that the Glasgow Group must have hit a very sensitive nerve.[7] The most telling response has been the broadcasters' suggestion that television news is inevitably limited in its explanatory power and that the full story is to be found in current affairs programmes. But of course the audience for news broadcasts is often ten times bigger than the audience for current affairs, so this would hardly outweigh any bias. In any case, current affairs programming is supposed to be designed to offer greater depth of coverage, not to act as an antidote to political partiality. That is why Birtism is not a counterweight to political bias.

A marginally more advanced complaint has come from Professor Alastair Hetherington (ex-*Guardian* editor and former Controller of BBC Scotland). Professor Hetherington's own content analyses of industrial relations have been rather slight, but he has used them to suggest that the bias critique is entirely wrong. During the 1984–5 coal dispute he attempted to disavow the critics of television news by demonstrating that its coverage devoted more airtime to the striking miners than than to their employers, the National Coal Board.[8] However, critics of the media have never disputed the repeated finding that workers tend to receive more airtime than employers. Indeed, it is the *invisibility* of key economic and investment decision-makers that is part of television's bias; the Left have for years bemoaned the lack of coverage of 'investment strikes', for instance. It is of course the quality not the quantity that must be the yardstick in this kind of research. A large amount of negative coverage is hardly something that anyone will have cause to celebrate.

The broadcasters did succeed in opening up the bias debate when ITN granted researcher Martin Harrison access to transcripts of the same news bulletins analysed in the early Glasgow Media Group studies. In his book *TV News: Whose Bias?* Harrison presents a series of criticisms of the group's methods and conclusions that focus on three areas of complaint.

The first of these is the group's belief that there is a 'dominant' view of society that is slavishly reproduced by the media. This might be termed the dominant 'ideology' – a set of ideas that are seen as natural and obvious, but which in fact serve to legitimate the *status quo*. Harrison not only rejects the view that the media do this, he refutes the whole notion of a dominant ideology. In this, I believe that he is wrong and the Glasgow Group are right. But in establishing his argument he makes the important point that the views and opinions attributed to the dominant group also seem to be rather widespread among other social groups, including workers and trade unionists.

For instance, the charge that the language of demand/offer and threaten/promise is biased seems rather weak when we consider that this is often just how trade unionists themselves talk. It may be that many views held by workers and trade unionists that are a part of the dominant ideology are widespread because of media influence. But that doesn't address the issue, since critics of news bias hold that the media distort the views of the public, regardless of where they came from in the first place.

Secondly, Harrison questions the group's conclusion that television news transmits a one-sided view of social conflict. He notes that their methodology is often rather impressionistic, relying on the presentation of argument with illustration as opposed to more scientific forms of content analysis. The problem here, of course, is that it is always possible to select those examples which best suit your argument, ignoring counter-evidence. But Harrison also argues that the group misinterpret some of their data. He quotes from *More Bad News* thus:

> In the phrase 'the strikers are demanding a pay rise of £10 per week' the strikers are alien to mankind in general – strikers are not you or me, they are somebody else. Thus when it is our strike, we are cut out of the message.

Harrison comments:

> The words 'alien to mankind in general', which might have been expected to confirm or illustrate the assertion do not in fact do so: instead they say something different and weaker . . . . Is it suggested that any use of the third person in news reporting treats those concerned as 'alien to mankind in general', or that third person accounts of any event in which we are involved . . . 'cut us out of the message' – or are these facts in some mysterious way peculiar to strikers?

Harrison concludes of the group's method: 'What they present is *their* preferred reading, without any demonstration that this was actually preferred by either the broadcasters or the audience.'

This points towards a third area that Harrison finds problematic – the question of audience interpretation. If academics like Harrison and the Glasgow Group can disagree on the meaning of television news, who can say how the television audience reacts? There is a paradox at the heart of the bias argument. For while it insists that television news is transmitting a 'dominant' view, it is always based on a quite different reading of the news from the one attributed to the audience! We know from audience research that people can react quite differently to the same message, depending on their predispositions. Therefore, any analysis of the media that bases itself on the assumption that television news has only *one* meaning is bound to be faced with limitations. An example is the question of interview settings. Why do the bias critics assume that everyone gives credence to someone sitting at a desk in a book-lined room? Many of us are immediately sceptical of anyone appearing in this setting! We might be more inclined to believe a worker outside a factory gate, on the grounds that s/he has experience of the issues s/he is talking about.

This brings us to another problem in the bias approach. Apparently groups throughout society believe that television and the media are biased against them. Fascists and neo-Nazis see a liberal/communist conspiracy against their ideas. Moralists and upholders of Victorian virtues such as Mary Whitehouse and her National Viewers and Listeners Association also see a permissive liberal bias. The Social Democratic Party (before it merged with the Liberals) also complained about bias, and on one occasion took the broadcasters to court to obtain more airtime for their party political broadcasts. And the most notable convert to the bias school of research with regard to television news is the Conservative Party, which launched a monitoring unit to detect anti-Tory bias in 1986. Tory Director of Communications Harvey Thomas even took time at the 1985 party conference to adopt some of the jargon of academic media research, accusing the media of anti-Conservative 'agenda setting'.

## TV news: striking the right balance?

Colin Sparks claims to perceive 'a new wave of "revisionist" writing about TV news' which attempts to let the broadcasters off the hook. Citing the research of Hetherington and Harrison alongside a report published by the Broadcasting Research Unit entitled *Television and the Miners' Strike*, Sparks initiated an important debate in the pages of *Media, Culture and*

*Society*.[9] The BRU's paper combines a year-long content analysis of TV news during the 1984–5 coal dispute with audience surveys designed to investigate public perception of the coverage. Their conclusions amount to a significant critique of the bias paradigm, since they believe that 'the content analysis and the public opinion surveys support the notion that "balance" was usually achieved' and that 'concerns that the media set the agenda for public perceptions of issues are not supported by our data'.[10] These findings are especially important given the 'test case' nature of the coal dispute. If bias is not present here, in one of the most bitter industrial disputes in British history, then surely it must be an invention of the Left?

However, it is worth noting that *Television and the Miners' Strike* makes two points that sustain the bias argument. First, it argues that there was a tendency for coverage to privilege social effects over causes. Second, it states that 'balance of ideas (such as the right to work – versus the right to strike) was less evident'.

*Television and the Miner's Strike* has itself been subject to a number of scathing critiques. Sparks suggests that this research is itself politically biased, and that the detailed findings of the work contradict the report's conclusions. This is also my view, and is buttressed by the fact that in the subsequent debate the authors do not, in my opinion, adequately meet the criticisms that are made of their work. You can assess the debate yourself by reading the report and the arguments that followed.

Perhaps the most serious and savage criticism that can be made of the bias argument is that it is mounted as a smoke screen designed to cover up other problems. 'Blaming the media', as Ian Connell calls it in an essay on media bias, can become an excuse for not addressing the real causes of unpopularity or indifference from union members or the general public. Television bias can thus be both a self-fulfilling prophesy (if you believe that the news is inevitably against you, what's the point in bothering with news management?) and a form of (self-)deception. There is a sense in which the perception of bias is actually comforting to some people, since it confirms their view of a media conspiracy (if the media hate us, we must be right!) and offers a painless explanation for political unpopularity. It is also a propaganda tool that can be used to divert attention away from the failings of politicians. These arguments against the bias paradigm come, surprisingly perhaps, from the Left, where the most sophisticated and challenging criticisms of the bias critique are usually to be found. The most damning review of the Glagow Group's work has come not from the broadcasters, but in a review of *More Bad News* written by Ian Connell and published in the Communist Party journal *Marxism Today*. Like Harrison, Connell first and most fundamentally takes issue with the view that conservative ideas are transmitted from the top to the bottom of society. In his review of *More Bad News*, he notes that the notion of wages-led inflation was widely held throughout the British labour movement: 'The basic economic ideology spoken of in *More Bad News* was not dominant simply because it was advanced by the politically powerful. It was dominant . . . because it framed the economic issues for . . . subordinate groups also.'[10]

The Glasgow Group argue that the broadcasters have failed to achieve balance, in that alternative and oppositional political and economic philosophies are largely absent from their agenda. Connell argues, on the other hand, that the broadcasters are only required to take account of the weight of public opinion holding these philosophies. So, for instance, while there may be a minority of citizens in the criminal fraternity who believe that it is right and proper to make a living by robbing banks, their views are not considered a suitable component in the balance of financial news. Perhaps it *should* be so, but this is not how balance has been understood. There are of course many political groups who hold competing explanations of the social and economic world who receive little or no sympathetic coverage on television news broadcasts – terrorists, fascists, anarchists, and revolutionary socialists are generally excluded by virtue of their lack of public support and/or their rejection of the rules of the game of political life in a parliamentary democracy.

Given that the broadcasters could not conceivably aim to reflect every viewpont in society, however unpopular, there is a sense in which they are legitimately biased. A former Director-General of the BBC, Sir Charles Curran, said as much when he commented:

> One of my senior editors said recently, in a phrase which I treasure: 'Yes, we are biased – biased in favour of parliamentary democracy.' And I agree with him. It is our business to contribute to the debate by making available to the widest general public the opinions of those who are directly engaged in it.[11]

Some will object that this does in fact reveal bias, towards those ideas which are viewed as 'legitimate' as opposed to those ideas that are not. I happen to agree with them. But that does not remove the central problem raised here in the clash between Connell and the Glasgow Group – namely, that 'impartiality' cannot possibly mean that all competing accounts of political, social, and economic events should receive equal and equitable coverage in television news, no matter how slight their popular currency.

Connell's objection to the Glasgow Group on this score is that they misread the terms of the broadcasters' right to broadcast, where obligations to observe '*due* impartiality' include a requirement to consider the numbers of people who give support or credence to the competing frameworks of explanation available in any given set of events. Therefore it becomes pointless to complain about 'bias' in coverage of inflation, when a large degree of parliamentary consensus did in fact exist on the question of the role of wages, extending into the trade union and labour movement itself. It is futile to bemoan 'bias' in coverage of Ireland, because bi-partisan policies adopted by government and opposition *are* adequately represented in television news. It becomes absurd to complain about bias in coverage of the Labour Left, when the parliamentary leadership of the Labour Party is itself orchestrating the anti-Left propaganda.

In other words, this argument states that television news does offer a balanced view, but it is one based on the limits of Parliamentary consensus.

## Bias and beyond

We need to be clear about the nature of these complaints. 'Bias' is not the opposite of 'truth'. All news reporting implies a point of view – in the selection of stories, the placement of cameras, the choice of locations, the selection of interviewees, and the content and tone of the language used by reporters and presenters. The real issue is whether the range of biases represented is fair. In other words, does it adequately reveal the range of points of view held by the public?

The debate between the Glasgow Media Group and its critics has been posed here as a very polarized one; indeed, this is often how it has been conducted. There is, however, some middle ground. As Richard Collins has suggested, it is feasible to accept the criticisms of the Glasgow Group's methodology, without rejecting all their findings. Collins is hostile to the Glasgow Group's methods, but he is still able to show that even Harrison's rather mild critique of ITN turns up evidence of bias, and that some of this is neglected in Harrison's analysis of his own data – the ITN transcripts. Harrison fails to note that, in a series of items about a SOGAT strike at Mirror Group Newspapers in 1975, ITN twice placed responsibility for the dispute with the union, not the employer who had sacked 1,750 members of its workforce. Collins concludes:

> It is an extraordinary omission that would demand at least qualification if not revision of his vindication of ITN. . . . The majority of the items [in the ITN transcripts] attribute responsibility for the dispute to workers, not employers. Harrison's account is no less open to criticism of selective attention to data than are those of the Glasgow Group.[12]

More fundamentally, while Connell may well be correct to suggest that television news adequately reflects the balance of parliamentary forces, that does not rule out bias, given that Parliament is in many ways an extremely unrepresentative institution, which reproduces imbalances of class, race, and gender that are evident throughout British society. It is one thing to say that broadcasting upholds the ideals of parliamentary democracy (as Sir Charles Curran states), but quite another to suggest that the broadcasters therefore take their political agenda solely from the existing balance of forces in a particular Parliament, or from the leadership of the mainstream political parties (Connell's argument).

It could be argued, following Connell's lead, that television news attempts to reflect the balance of opinion in public debate. But that would not rule out bias, partly because 'public opinion' is often understood in relation to a generally rightwing press (which frequently funds the opinion polls) and partly because we know that some groups debate their problems more openly than others. Even if television does 'reflect' the form these debates take in parliamentary democracy it is in the nature of these institutions that the resulting coverage can still suffer from bias. Journalists will find it easier to obtain stories on more open organizations, where on-going debate can be parleyed into the dramatic action on which they need to hang stories (the Labour Party, trade unions, the Liberal Democrats) than organizations that control access and information more tightly (the Conservative Party, the police and armed forces, private companies). Conservative politicians in the liberal democracies of the west have repeatedly made exactly this point about media coverage of European and North American nations *vis-à-vis* the Soviet Union and eastern bloc countries.

There is another area where the Harrison and Connell critiques do not quite meet the point of the bias argument. This concerns the language used on television news. Connell and Harrison object that the Glasgow Group's charge of bias on the grounds of the imbalanced use of terms like 'offer/demand' and 'promise/reject' (and in the use of phrases such as 'the miner's strike') is phony – because this is how workers and trade unionists actually speak about such disputes. But this does not meet the point. Television news is nowhere charged with a responsibility to reproduce the actual language used by the protagonists in political and industrial affairs. (Journalists spend much of their professional lives *improving* upon the language used by elite figures in public affairs, after all, when they write up interviews. And television usually censors obscene or racist language.) So while Harrison and Connell are correct to alert our attention to the presence of 'biased' linguistic formulations outside television, that doesn't let the broadcasters off the hook at all.

Furthermore, while the arguments about differing audience interpretations should lead to scepticism about *any* 'scientific' analysis of television texts (be it sociological or semiological), this does not totally invalidate those critics who see bias. It may well be that the Glasgow Group are picking up *one set of readings*. My experience of teaching trade unionists about news tells me that the Glasgow work certainly resonates very strongly amongst committed labour movement activists and is often greeted with a great degree of recognition amongst working-class students generally, regardless of activism. Even if it is true that the bias critique is only one way of reading of the news, it is sufficiently widespread to give cause for concern. Critics of the bias argument will say that if bias is *perceived*, then it doesn't matter, since it can have no effect. The answer to this is two-pronged. First, those activists who have access to other frameworks of meaning that override news bias are also surely entitled to news from their point of view, just like middle-of-the-road uncommitted viewers. At present, there is no news for viewers committed to the trade union movement, and/or those to the left of centre. That, surely, is what the Glasgow Group's work is actually saying, and it is a perfectly legitimate complaint. Secondly, we have no idea what the effect of news bias is upon viewers who do not have access to frameworks of meaning other than those provided by television news. It does not imply any commitment to simplistic 'hypodermic needle' theories of media effects, or prestructuralist analysis of 'monosemic' texts (where texts are assumed to have only one essential meaning, for everyone), to suggest that there are probably *some* effects for *some* viewers.

It has become fashionable to regard the bias paradigm as outdated on two grounds, each of which is bogus. First it is suggested that all bias critiques are based on some form of conspiracy theory. This is not so. It is quite possible to argue for non-conspiratorial explanations of news bias. Indeed, it is possible to argue that autonomy from social leverage is an *explanation* for bias, since journalists come from class backgrounds that don't lend themselves to an understanding of working-class culture, and are usually imbued with a fairly vague political liberalism which is hostile both to socialist and Thatcherite ideals. Left to its own devices, television news would be more than capable of all kinds of biases.

One area of unconscious bias obviously derives from news values themselves. One of the classic values employed in selecting news is 'negativity', and when this is combined with 'frequency' (news has to be as 'new' as the publication or broadcast presenting it) the effect is often of a barrage of bad things happening in the world which seem to have no rhyme or reason. One of the Conservative Party's complaints has been that when they close a hospital ward, that is news; but when they build a new hospital, that isn't news. Hence broadcasting creates an image of a heartless, uncaring Conservative government, through the bias of news selection. This is exactly the argument that trade unionists have been making for years about strikes. When we go to work, they say, that isn't news. When we go on strike, that *is* news. Hence broadcasting creates an image of a lazy workforce willing to strike at the drop of a shop steward's hat. Here, bias in news values themselves creates the problem.

A second area of philosophical objection to the term 'bias' arises when it is argued that all media language is 'constructed' and that therefore any methodology basing itself on the complaint of 'distortion' is innocently mimetic. Media representations are not 'reflections', say these critics, (this is true), and so the complaint that the reflection is imperfect must be misplaced (which is not necessarily true). It is quite plausible to believe that all media images are constructed and still maintain that some constructions are more truthful than others. Surely there are competing explanations of social reality, and surely all factual statements are also statements of value. But none of this means that there are not real events in the actual world that do take place and unreal events in the minds of policemen, politicians, and Coal Board officials that do not take place. These arguments should not prevent us from noticing that some explanations receive more attention and validation than others.

The accusation of 'bias' does not have to be epistemologically naive or methodologically unsound, and some critics of these charges may well be accused in their turn of oversimplifying the case made for it. It is certainly true that left-leaning seekers of bias have not always been as rigorous as they might, and that some arguments made against television news are quite invalid. It is also true that if there *is* a rightwing or middle-of-the-road case against television news, it has yet to show itself in any body of scholarly works.

For the time being, the broadcasters seem content to note that they are often shot by both sides, with Thatcherites and socialists complaining about bias. They sometimes take solace in this, since they seem to believe that when each side complains, they must be getting it 'right'. The broadcasters prefer not to hear that this very assumption, based as it is on the notion that the 'truth' exists somewhere in the middle of every debate, is itself a forceful political bias. Moderation remains the 'extremist' political dogma of television news.


## Notes

My thanks to John Field for his comments on an earlier version of this article.

1 Asa Briggs, *The History of Broadcasting in the United Kingdom*, vol. 4: *Sound and Vision*, Oxford: Oxford University Press, 1979.
2 Grace Wyndham Goldie, *Facing the Nation: Television and Politics, 1936–75*, London: Bodley Head, 1977.
3 Neil Postman, *Amusing Ourselves to Death: Public Discourse in the Age of Show Business*, London: Penguin, 1985.
4 Quoted in Philip Schlesinger, op. cit. in Further reading.
5 See the arguments of television news producer David Cox, 'A new life for TV news: revitalisation can only come from outside', *Listener*, 31 December 1987.
6 In addition to *Really Bad News* (see Further reading), the Glasgow University Media Group's books are: *Bad News* (London: Routledge & Kegan Paul, 1976), *More Bad News* (London: Routledge & Kegan Paul, 1980), and *War and Peace News* (Milton Keynes: Open University Press, 1985).
7 See the review of press coverage in Gillian Skirrow, '*More Bad news* – a review of the reviews', *Screen*, vol. 21, no. 2 (Summer 1980).
8 See Hetherington's contribution to a debate at the 1984 Edinburgh International Television Conference, reprinted in 'Scargill takes on the telly men', *New Socialist*, October 1984.
9 See Colin Sparks, 'Striking results' and John Brown, Robin McGregor, and Guy Cumberbatch, 'Tilting at windmills: an attempted murder by misrepresentation', *Media, Culture and Society*, vol. 9, no. 3 (1987); Martin Barker, 'News bias and the miners' strike: the debate continues . . .', and Guy Cumberbatch *et al.*, 'Arresting knowledge: a response to the debate about *TV and the Miners' Strike*', *Media, Culture and Society*, vol. 10, no. 1 (1988); Greg Philo, '*Television and the Miners' Strike* – a note on method', *Media, Culture and Society*, vol. 10, no. 4 (1988).
10 Guy Cumberbatch, Robin McGregor, and John Brown, with David Morrison, *Television and the Miners' Strike*, London: Broadcasting Research Unit, 1986, p. 135.
11 Ian Connell, review of *More Bad News*, *Marxism Today*, August 1980.
12 Quoted in Stuart Hall, Ian Connell, and Lidia Curti, 'The "Unity" of Current Affairs Television', *Working Papers in Cultural Studies* no. 9, Birmingham: Centre for Contemporary Cultural Studies, University of Birmingham, 1976.
13 Richard Collins, '*Bad News* and bad faith: the story of a political controversy', *Journal of Communication*, Autumn 1980.

# Further reading

Connell, Ian, 'Blaming the media', in Len Masterman (ed.), *TV Mythologies*, London: Comedia, 1985.

Glasgow University Media Group, *Really Bad News*, London: Writers and Readers Co-operative, 1982.

Harrison, Martin, *TV News: Whose Bias?*, London: Policy Journals, 1985.

Schlesinger, Philip, *Putting Reality Together: BBC News*, London: Constable, 1978.

# 4 POINTS OF VIEW

## Rosalind Brunt

I want in this chapter to indicate what's involved in 'asking the right questions' about the television text. In particular, I'll be drawing on studies that have adopted contemporary Marxist, linguistic, and cultural theories to provide a new vocabulary for media research. I cannot explore much of the intellectual 'underpinnings' of these theories, so I've indicated some of their sources in the notes.[1] My starting point will be to mobilize some of these new terms and then take the breakfast television programme, *Good Morning Britain*, as a concrete example of the sort of questions we might usefully ask about 'pictures of the world'.

### Texts and ideologies

The new research paradigm has been characterized by Stuart Hall as a concern with 'the ideological effect' of television:[2] how ideologies work in and through television. It is based on a recognition that television communicates meanings, values, and beliefs. These communications are not just individual 'matters of opinion', purely personal points of view, but messages that are socially produced in particular circumstances and made culturally available as shared explanations of how the world works. In other words, they are 'ideologies', explanatory systems of belief. I think a researcher needs to approach them by asking three preliminary questions. First, how do ideologies work as 'configurations' of meaning: how do they hang together and crystallize *as* particular systems of belief? Secondly, who believes them? How are they interpreted as 'collective representations' of particular social groups? Finally, how are they located? What are the historical circumstances that gave rise to these sets of ideas or 'world views', and what are the continuing material conditions, the political, economic, and institutional orders that support their existence?

Having a general notion of 'ideology' that alerts the researcher to these three aspects of configuration, collective representation, and context requires a methodological approach based on an 'interpretative explanation' of the television message. Because the 'ideological effect' is about the giving and taking of meanings and how both producers and receivers of messages 'make sense of' what is culturally on offer, the task of the researcher is to interpret the 'value-orientation' of the messages and render their ideological configurations intelligible and explicit. How this has typically been done is by the method of 'textual reading', concentrating on individual television messages – say, one programme in a series. This is then treated as a 'text' to be 'read'/interpreted in terms of its wider ideological significance.[3]

The choice of taking just one programme as a 'text' is not only a recognition of the sheer amount of time it takes to make any detailed reading. It is also an acknowledgement that, whilst each programme is unique and unrepeatable, it is, nevertheless, precisely to the extent that it is communicating, composed of recognizable and understandable provinces of meaning. In just the same way that all 'news' is in some sense also 'olds', any television message can be seen as having some 'typical' characteristic or representative significance. The question of 'point of view' is crucial here. For a 'reading' requires both that the 'angle' of the research is made clear – just *what* is being highlighted as 'significant'? – and that the 'text' is explained in terms of the particular perspectives that make it meaningful to its audiences. Using the one example of *Good Morning Britain*, I want to demonstrate how such a reading might work. What follows then is not itself a detailed textual interpretation; it's rather a sort of checklist, or notes for guidance for examining television in terms of ideological effect.

## Institutional context

*Good Morning Britain* is a programme transmitted every weekday between 7.00 and 9.00 a.m. by TV-AM, an Independent Television company granted a franchise in 1983. It is a 'magazine' programme, hosted by two presenters, interspersed with half-hourly news and weather bulletins and containing a mix of news, commentary, and entertainment features.

In my view, an adequate textual analysis of any television programme should first be related to some account of its *political economy*: that is, a study of the economic context of production that draws out the political

61

consequences of ownership and control. In the case of *Good Morning Britain*, this means addressing issues like: the commercial history of the television station (for example, TV-AM's drastic changes of management and ownership; its conflict with the unions over new working practices); the relationship with the regulatory body of ITV, the Independent Broadcasting Authority (the IBA's continued attempts to insert more 'hard news' content and maintain broadcast standards against the station's commercial pull to be more 'entertainment-led'); the role of advertising (the need for high audience ratings to maximize the advertising revenue which is ITV's main income, combined with the 'market-penetration' of specific 'target' audiences like schoolchildren and parents of babies and toddlers); the publicity context (the programme as feature of other media via tabloid and women's magazine journalism, particularly the 'star' treatment of presenters and the packaging of Anne Diamond – 'I think of myself as a commodity' – and her status as 'Britain's most famous unmarried mum').

Such elements of a political economy serve as important indicators of how a programme works as a *commodity*. *Good Morning Britain* is a product which, in classic Marxist terms, has both a 'use value' (it offers its audiences, according to the standard British broadcasting formula, 'information, entertainment and education'), and also an 'exchange value' (it is a product offered on the marketplace for money). The inherent problem of commodity production is that the moneymaking exchange value may predominate over the programme-making use value. Indeed, that, in summary, is the whole 'troubled history' of TV-AM. At the same time, the programme content of *Good Morning Britain* cannot just be 'read off' in any simple way by reference to the overriding concern of its station managers to make money by cost-cutting and audience-maximization strategies.

Political economy militates against an 'innocent' reading of the television text by pointing to what sets its limits: the key institutional parameters within which the message is produced. But a researcher has to be careful to avoid any 'vulgar' economic determinism in making this connexion; that is, to beware of seeing content as straightforwardly and overwhelmingly determined by its production context.

### Analysing the text

Let's assume that a researcher approaches a textual analysis of *Good Morning Britain* already sensitively attuned to the likely implications of its commodity function. The next task would be some 'gross reckoning' of programme items to get an overall sense of the programme's agenda. This would involve watching a run of individual programmes for comparative purposes and doing some preliminary categorization and quantification of content. It would then require giving some evidence of this, as a demonstration of accuracy, before moving to the third stage, the interpretation of a single programme. In my case, any illustration of this second task of basic *content analysis* will have to be taken on trust!

The *Good Morning Britain* that I've chosen as 'typical' was transmitted on 27 October 1987. In addition to its regular informational bulletins, the day's programmes can be roughly categorized as a mixture of 'serious', news-related items and 'lighthearted' personality/showbiz items, as follows: 'serious' discussion of a forthcoming parliamentary bill to restrict abortion; a conference on the electronic 'tagging' of prisoners; the 25-year sentence passed on 'an IRA bombmaker' the previous day; 'lighthearted' interviews with an actor on a current children's programme (Jon Pertwee), and with a Cockney boxer-turned-film-celebrity ('Nosher' Powell); plus regular features like the *Popeye* cartoon and 'access' slots like *Popshots* (photographs of viewers combined with a current hit song) and *Post Host* (viewers' letters compiled by a celebrity presenter). There were two additional items that combined the elements of both these categories in terms of 'soft news': speculation about the marriage of the Prince and Princess of Wales, and an examination of a new portrait of the current members of the House of Commons.

Now to ask what in the world any of this list of contents might actually 'mean', the programme has to be approached as if it's a most peculiar phenomenon indeed. For interpretative work is not the same as ordinary viewing which is likely to be casual and routine and take place in an environment full of distractions. Textual analysis requires some degree of critical distance or 'making strange' in order to 'deconstruct' a programme, unpack its constituent elements and work out exactly what is going on. This is because all television programmes inhabit deeply familiar terrains – which is what makes them so effective as mass communications – and as viewers we usually 'know where we are with them'. As interpreters of programmes, we both have to draw on our own familiarity with the culture and the knowledge gained from routine television watching, whilst at the same time 'defamiliarizing' a specific text by recognizing, highlighting, and spelling out precisely those elements it takes for granted, which are presumed to be so obvious to all viewers that they almost 'go without saying'.

To get at any programme's underlying assumptions, a productive starting point is the question of *mode of address*: how is the programme speaking to its viewers? who is the programme appealing to? what 'tone of voice' or 'accent' does it adopt towards its assumed audience? A first consideration might be the programme's title. Unusually for British television, *Good Morning Britain* takes the form of a direct address to viewers. Its bold claim is that the audience is not merely a large number of British people but an entire national formation: their interests are, by definition alone, the national interest. *GMB*'s title addresses its audience as 'you', but its presenters use 'you' and 'we' pronouns interchangeably in a way that brings the unseen audience 'out there' into the programme's ambit 'in here', the television studio. How personal pronouns are used is crucial to establishing a common identity between presenter and audience. The use of 'we' means both that 'we' the presenters are just like 'you' the ordinary viewer, really, but also that we = you = Britain in the sense of 'we in this country would all agree, wouldn't we?'

The way a programme implicates its views in its address is reinforced by its *forms of presentation* – time slot, format, continuity, studio setting, camera conventions, etc. To take one example, the basic studio setting of *GMB* is large sofas, table for coffee-serving, picture window 'view', monitor for beaming in news inserts and filmed extracts. What this 'says' is informality and relaxation before the start of a 'working' day.

But little of visual interest happens on the set apart from guests and presenters changing places on the sofas. The main element is verbal: the programme is held together by talk. The talk repertoire is primarily conversational, as instanced in bantering between guests and presenters, repeated first-naming, effusive thanks, informal comments, anecdotes, and references to media gossip. The programme's predominant tone of voice is one of chatty informality as presenters manage a constant interplay between studio conversation across the sofas and appeals to the viewer via the convention of direct address to camera. It is most evident in the continuity links and handovers:

7.58 a.m. (Fade out *Popshots*; fade in 'The Weathergirl' dancing to *Popshots* hit in front of smiley-type weather chart).
*Trish Williams*: (to camera) One of my favourite bands! Well, let's see if that'll get into the Top Ten. Well, the weather. Although the temperatures are certainly getting up there. . . . The weather is moving up, actually, from the Mediterranean. They're having *incredible* temperatures there. . . . Now back to Richard.
*Richard Keys*: Trish, thank you very much indeed. (To camera) This is *Good Morning Britain*. It's exactly 8.00 a.m. Time for us to say a very

good morning to Gordon Honeycombe (turns to monitor behind sofa; fade-in GH).

*Gordon Honeycombe:* (turns to RK) Morning Richard. (To camera) First the headlines on Wednesday 27 October. . . That's the news. It's 9 minutes past 8. Here's Anne.

*Anne Diamond:* (to GH fading-out) Thank you. (To camera) And as you heard Gordon say, the IRA's top bombmaker, Gilbert McNamee, starts a 25-year jail sentence today. . . .

Through the conversational interchanges of 'you' and 'me' and 'us' and the other forms of address and presentation, what is happening here is that *points of identification* are being established with viewers in ways which help to secure consent for the views expressed in the programme. Again, care needs to be taken in approaching identification. It is all too easy to make the workings of ideology appear like the processes of propaganda. But the conversational strategies in play here are no exercise in deliberate manipulation. It is rather that they are, in all senses, 'inviting' and 'engaging' the viewer to go along with the values of the programme.

So what might these values and perspectives be? Having examined how various mechanisms of viewer identification operate, a textual analysis might then proceed to the specifics of naming some ideological configurations operating in particular programme items. I will briefly take three examples from *GMB* to indicate the sort of issues that arise in attempting to 'read for ideology'.

First, I will take the discussion of 'the IRA's top bombmaker', because it constituted the 'hardest' of the news-related features. It was placed second in the preceding news bulletin and Anne Diamond then opened discussion of it by referring to the headlines of the daily newspaper in front of her, interspersed with her own comments:

*Anne Diamond:* . . . This morning's front pages reflect [the story]. *Times:* 'IRA graduate who became a bombmaker.' He was, of course, a science graduate. It would appear he was killing people while he was studying. . . . *The Daily Mail* called him 'The Student of Death'. . . . *The Daily Express:* 'IRA bomber may have killed 80', but the *Sun* says he's responsible for 90 deaths and *Today* there: '90 Victims of IRA Assassin.' McNamee's bombs are said to be also responsible for up to 90 other deaths in mainland Britain and Northern Ireland, as these papers reflect. But does his arrest mean the IRA have lost their ability to repeat such outrages? Well, we're joined this morning by Chris Ryder, who's Northern Ireland correspondent of *The Sunday Times*. Good morning.

*Chris Ryder*: Good morning.

*AD*: What seems insidious, I think, to a lot of people who have heard the story yesterday or watched it unfold in court, was that this man was devising people's deaths while he was studying at university.

*CR*: Well, there has, unfortunately, been a terrorist cell operating for some time in Queen's University, Belfast. . . .

*AD*: So, in Northern Ireland the university campus is still a hotbed of –

*CR*: (intervening) The university campus has been the hotbed ever since the civil rights movement. . . . And, unfortunately, in a divided society, students are very interested in politics and the future of the country. And that's reflected in the activities of the university – apart from the normal, academic, er, pursuits.

*AD*: McNamee is clearly, what they would call in the business, a very big fish to catch. He's going to be a very difficult man to keep behind bars, isn't he?

The interview concludes with speculation that the IRA already have trained replacement bombmakers:

*AD*: So we should, in a way, take no comfort from these headlines?

*CR*: Oh no. The IRA is a sleeping dog that will be barking again.

*AD*: And Christmas is coming –

*CR*: Yes, Christmas. The security forces won't be complacent at all. But the IRA is always probing for a pinpoint that'll allow them to cause some atrocity.

*AD*: Chris Ryder, we'll leave it there. Thank you very much. (To camera) We'll take a short break and afterwards we'll be looking again at the Prince and Princess of Wales and particularly how other countries reflect *our* news about them. We'll be having a look at that lovely frock she was wearing last night. We'll be back in a minute. (Caption: *8.15. Coming Up: Royal Marriage.*)

Any investigation of point of view starts with a basic question about *the legitimation of the message*: says who? In the bombmaker item a number of claims are made; how are they legitimated? That is, who is making the claims? with what authority and on whose behalf? In this case, an ideological reading would note, for example, the extent to which television's agenda is set by the press. *GMB* offers both verbal and visual reinforcement of the newspaper angle because both the preceding news item and Anne Diamond's display of the tabloid press featured the same picture of McNamee in graduate gown and cap. The story was thus

66

framed in terms of 'The Student of Death' approach, recalling a still familiar 1970s image of students as political deviants. This was linked to the extreme deviancy of the IRA and made ultra-devious by apparent respectability (the degree-day picture implying conformism but, of course, fooling everybody). Further, when Anne Diamond refers to public opinion she automatically identifies it with the perspective of the press: no other evidence is offered of what the British public's attitude might be.

But central to broadcasting's ideology is the convention that, unlike the press, broadcasters remain impartial and do not express their own opinions. If Anne Diamond can't take sides, the only position she can legitimately adopt is that of speaking for 'all' or 'most' of 'us', the viewers, the British public ('what seems insidious . . . to a lot of people'), but because she has no independent means of knowledge, she must offer a qualification, speculatively phrased (the insertion of 'I think').

She is, however, only asking the questions. It is the interviewee who is the expert. His qualification to speak derives from his knowledge of the field – actually 'being there' – and the prestige of his paper. And although he is allowed to be partisan in the press, it is assumed that on television he will obey the code of professionalism and appear as both dispassionate witness and informed commentator.

What is striking about the ensuing interview is the extent to which both interviewer and interviewee share the same framework of assumptions. Although Anne Diamond adopts an interrogative and speculative tone on behalf of viewers, she never actually *questions* any of what the expert says. From within this shared perspective, the interview is conducted primarily at the level of pragmatic and technical detail: it is 'about' ways in which national security can best be maintained. The ideological 'effect' is that viewers are invited to 'take' the IRA from the state's point of view, as primarily a matter of 'law and order'.

To make such an interpretation is not, however, the same thing as accusing television of 'bias'. On the contrary, an ideological reading imputes a degree of *complexity* to the message. The identification of viewers' with state's interests is not automatic, nor necessarily easily achieved. It depends on what Stuart Hall calls considerable 'ideological labour', whereby a number of perspectives are aligned, viz: viewers' interests = tabloid press = public opinion = the presenter = the expert = codes of professionalism = national interest = interests of state (security).

However, there is no guarantee that all the points of view in a text will always align that neatly. There are likely to be problematic 'gaps' in the account, disjunctures, and possible contradictions. So in this interview there are several areas which are hardly legitimate, despite legitimation. For instance, the use of the passive voice where agency is deleted ('bombs are said' – by whom?); the appearance of the anonymous 'they' and assertions open to challenge on the evidence ('a terrorist cell' – why not investigated?) Above all, from what perspective is interest in the future of your country and in politics 'unfortunate'? These unasked and unanswered questions leave the interview 'open' for audiences to form some alternative interpretations. It is by no means stitched up for the *status quo*.

But neither is it so open that it will admit of any variety of equivalent interpretations, as the liberal notion of broadcasting based on the model of pluralism and balance of views maintains. Rather, as Hall suggests, ideological labour creates *preferred meanings*. Certain themes will be 'preferred' and proffered by the programme to the audience as an explanatory cluster, a repertoire of opinion that will have 'the overall tendency of making things "mean" within the sphere of the dominant ideology'. What Hall is identifying here is an active process, a continual construction and reconstruction of particular views of the world which *tend* towards the reproduction of the *status quo*. And the 'labour' involved is not the clever political manipulation of 'bias' but the constant engagement and 'negotiation' with an audience in ways which effectively win their consent.

From this standpoint, it is irrelevant what views a presenter like Anne Diamond actually holds or whether her interview is overtly or covertly partisan. Rather, ideological effectiveness is achieved precisely to the degree that the interview maintains its professionalism and in the smoothest, friendliest manner is then able to make an apparently effortless transition ('we'll take a short break') to other items of assumed equivalent interest to the viewer ('we'll be looking again at the Prince and Princess of Wales').

All television programmes impute a degree of cultural familiarity to their viewers and ideological readings need to be alert to what *common stocks of knowledge*[4] are assumed to be available to 'all' viewers. For *GMB* it is taken for granted that the audience will be familiar with current tabloid press speculation about royalty and that they will therefore fully comprehend a caption that says only 'Coming Up: Royal Marriage'.

I take this item as my second example because, while a royal marriage has no real material bearing on anybody else's lives and can in no way be designated 'hard news', it nevertheless features in the media as the type of story which has the important *symbolic* function of expressing something about 'the state of the nation'. In particular, it plays a crucial part in the media's construction of national ideologies, of 'Britishness'.

In *GMB*'s royal marriage item, 'Britishness' is defined in relation to what we can 'all' be assumed to know about other countries and what they think of 'our' Royal Family. The feature is conducted as a discussion between the two presenters and British correspondents of Australian and American television companies, concerning how they are covering the current speculation. Much of the discussion functions as journalistic insider talk, conducted in professional jargon, about 'the natural position of the story', 'heads', 'leads', and 'station bosses' – to which we, as 'ordinary viewers', are given 'privileged' access, as if we're eavesdropping on the conversation. At the same time, the feature is also telling the national audience that we're already privileged because we're British rather than American or Australian. These are two of the initial questions from the presenters:

> *Richard Keys*: Um, are Americ— of course, it's almost a naive question – is America, are Americans, interested in the Royals? Of course they are, aren't they?. . .

> *Anne Diamond*: Do you think American people are fond of speculation? I mean, they always like talking about the Royal Family very much, but do you think they like this sort of speculation or find it distasteful? Some people in this country are beginning to turn against the press.

The item ends by recalling the earlier news item:

> *RK*: Well, the Princess, as we mentioned, was out at the gala ball last night. On her own. Dressed *beautifully*, I have to say. We can have a look at her now (repeated news film). What are you going to make of last night's appearance?
> *Australian broadcaster*: Well, in Australia, every Australian woman watches what she wears. The way she wears her hair, her make-up, they copy Princess Di. And I'd say by tomorrow morning half the women in Australia will have their hair swept up like that. . . .
> *AD*: What about Americans: Do they follow Diana very carefully?
> *American broadcaster*: Not like that, no. There's not a daily report of fashions and hairstyles.
> *AD*: More sceptical, are they, the Americans, than the Australians?
> *American*: It's just that we don't have as much time, I guess, for some of the less important news.
> *AD*: You've got bigger problems!? (laughter)
> *American*: I guess we do! (all laugh; end of item).

The tone here is 'thank goodness we're British!' It works in a way that both acknowledges Britain's inferior world status (*vis-à-vis* America, for instance) but ultimately decides in favour of Britishness, as if to say: at least we've got the (always interesting and culturally superior) Royal Family!

This message is effective to the extent of what is not said. For instance, the purpose and function of a royal family in a modern state forms no part of the discussion. The *omissions* and *silences* of a message may be as significant in constructing a 'preferred meaning' as its overt content. In this feature, the insistence on the obvious and taken-for-granted ('of course'), as well as the absence of any reference to the existence of the Royal Family as in any way problematic, contributes to a point of view of 'us the British' as both complacent and deferential to the existing institutional order.


## Who is addressed?

The issue of how the viewer is 'constructed' by the programme leads to my third example and final question. I think that it should always be asked: 'Who does this programme think the viewer(s) is/are?' This involves picking up the initial questions of modes of address, presentation and identification, but it is also a reference to *subject position*: how are viewers ideologically 'placed' in the programme and according to what procedures? The notion of 'positioning' involves a theory of ideology as working in a double movement, as indicated in the two contradictory meanings of 'subject'.[5] The programme invites us as 'subjects' who are free agents in control of our actions to 'subject ourselves' to a given view of the world and our (subordinate) place in it.

How this double and contradictory process works is indicated in the final item on *GMB*. This is a regular feature, *Post Host*, where a celebrity presenter (Gyles Brandreth, a regular host and guest of broadcast panel shows) suggests a topic for viewers' letters and reads out a selected response, together with comments from himself, the presenters, and any remaining guests on the sofa. The current topic is 'philosophical sayings':

> *Gyles Brandreth*: (To camera) After yesterday's amiable antics, you find us in much quieter, and, er, a more philosophical mood. In recent weeks, you've been sending us sage sayings, nuggets of gold, pearls of wisdom, and they come in all shapes and sizes . . . . This from (?) of Markfield Leicestershire: 'This saying graced my office wall for many years and confounded some of the most intelligent: "A wise monkey is

a monkey who doesn't monkey with another's monkey.'" Isn't that lovely?

*Presenters and guests*: Very good! Um, it's deep too!

*GB*: (?)from Horsham offers another profound and rather more provocative thought for the day: 'In order to live freely and happily you must sacrifice boredom. It is not always an easy sacrifice'. . . . Nick Robertson of Kenilworth, Warwickshire, has found philosophy in the cricket field: 'I think it was Lord Mancroft who said, "Cricket is a game which the British, not being a spiritual people, had to invent, in order to have some concept of eternity."'

*Presenters and guests*: Marvellous! Rather droll, isn't it?

The sequence contains thirteen sayings from viewers and concludes:

*GB*: But the last word has to go to Postbag's Personal Padre, the Reverend (?) of Gwent, whose contribution is a little verse entitled *Don't Quit*: 'Success is failure turned inside out/The silver tint of the clouds of doubt/And you never can tell how close you are/It may be near when it seems afar/So, stick to the fight when you're hardest hit./It's when things go wrong that you mustn't quit.' (To camera) But it's *you*, the *viewer* (arms out-stretched to camera) who always have the last word, so do write to us here. You know the address don't you?

What *GMB* tells its viewers is that this is your programme because you participate in it and have a controlling voice ('the last word'). Viewers are invited to join in the programme, but the agenda is already set. 'Having your say' amounts to being free to say anything, so long as it's wise sayings, a repetition of the already familiar and obvious categories of common sense: a bit jokey, a bit 'deep', but nothing that's going to stop the show. *GMB*'s invitation to viewers, its address to them as an audience of British people, does not arise from the terrain of the new, the difficult or the challenging. For 'you' are hardly going to change the world; the point is to know your place within it.

Television's subject positioning is about literally putting viewers in their place by assigning them a role in the world for which their consent is secured. So a programme that says, 'Good morning Britain', speaks to a nation composed of ordinary, homely folk who aren't causing any bother and who, indeed, are flattered to be noticed in the first place. It is an appeal to subordination that uses 'our' language, 'our' tone of voice, in the nicest, jolliest way to include us, at the very moment that it actually excludes us from power. In Richard Hoggart's phrase, it disenfranchises by 'unbending the springs of action'.[6]

In this brief outline, I've been offering a vocabulary of terms and some questions to indicate how various components of a textual, interpretative analysis can work to unpack the ways in which an ideological configuration, a point of view, is constructed. As Weber remarked, 'all knowledge of cultural reality is always knowledge from a particular point of view'.[7] For this reason, he said, researchers must be explicit about where they're coming from, what questions they're asking, and why, in order to make accessible their criteria for selecting certain configurations and not others, and to provide adequate documentary evidence for their choice.

Weber stressed that this was all the more important precisely because the object of study, cultural reality, was itself already and always implicated in meanings and values, crisscrossed with points of view. Only by spelling out their own angle, their own interpretation of existing interpretations, could researchers avoid the charge of sloppy subjectivism, the ultimate put-down of, 'well, of course, that's only *your* point of view'.

More orthodox social science has always accused interpretative analysis of subjectivism and consequently dismissed the whole terrain of ideological meanings as just too messy to be capable of any rigorous analysis in the first place. Hence, the constant temptation to retreat to the securities of behavioural models and the conventional notion of media 'effects'. But in *my* view, this is not the time for any theoretical backsliding.

## Notes

1 Among texts that have been particularly influential for the new model of media research are, e.g., L. Althusser, 'Ideology and the state', in *Lenin and Philosophy and Other Essays*, London: New Left Books, 1971; R. Barthes, *Mythologies*, London: Cape, 1972; A. Gramsci, *Selections from Prison Notebooks*, London: Lawrence & Wishart, 1971; V.N. Volosinov, *Marxism and the Philosophy of Language*, New York: Seminar Press, 1973.

2 Hall, op. cit. in Further reading. Also S. Hall, 'Encoding and decoding', in Hall *et al.* (eds), *Culture, Media, Language*, London: Hutchinson, 1980; and 'The rediscovery of "ideology": return of the repressed in the media studies', in M. Gurevitch *et al.* (eds), *Culture, Society and the Media*, London: Methuen, 1982.

3 'Interpretative explanation' and 'value-orientation' derive from *Verstehen* sociology developed in the early twentieth century by Max Weber (*Verstehen* = 'understanding'). The method of 'interpretative explanation' is elaborated in his influential essays, 'Objectivity in the social sciences and social policy' and 'The logic of the cultural sciences', in M. Weber, *Methodology of the Social Sciences*, New York: Free Press, 1949.

4 The notion of 'stocks of knowledge' is one first developed by the phenomenologist, Alfred Schutz, and elaborated by P. Berger and T. Luckmann in *The Social Construction of Reality*, Harmondsworth: Penguin, 1971. See especially their chapter, 'Legitimation'.
5 See Althusser, op. cit., for a theoretical approach to the notion of 'subject'.
6 See the chapter, 'Unbending the springs of action', in R. Hoggart, *The Uses of Literacy*, London: Penguin, 1958.
7 Weber, op. cit., p. 81.

## Further reading

Eco, Umberto, 'Towards a semiotic inquiry into the television message', *Working Papers in Cultural Studies*, no. 3, Birmingham: Centre for Contemporary Cultural Studies, University of Birmingham, 1972.
Hall, Stuart, 'Culture, media and "the ideological effect"', in James Curran *et al.* (eds), *Mass Communication and Society*, London: Edward Arnold, 1977.
Masterman, Len (ed.), *TV Mythologies*, London: Comedia, 1985.

# 5 F FOR FAKE?
## FRICTION OVER FACTION
*Paul Kerr*

Drama documentary, documentary drama, dramatized documentary, docudrama, dramadoc, faction, reconstruction. . . call it what you will – and it has been called more names than any other television form in its time – programmes which blend the devices of factual and fictional TV are often in the headlines and have even led, on occasion, to questions in the House of Commons. From Fleet Street to Downing Street, from the Home Office to the Foreign Office, programmes like *Cathy Come Home* and *The War Game* in the 1960s, *Law and Order* and *Days of Hope* in the 1970s, and *Death of a Princess* and *The Monocled Mutineer* in the 1980s have been a perennial problem for British broadcasting. And they have been treated accordingly: *The War Game* was banned for twenty years; *Scum* was suppressed, remade for the cinema, and subsequently (but unsuccessfully) prosecuted when screened by Channel 4; *Death of a Princess* was held responsible for a full-blown diplomatic incident, the screening of *The Monocled Mutineer* led to another bout of BBC-bashing by Norman Tebbit, and most recently *Tumbledown* also caused public controversy. But such programmes are not always so explosive – and that fact is far too easily forgotten in the wake of whatever is the latest 'controversy'.

This essay, however, is less concerned with either parliamentary or press fulminations about drama documentary (henceforth DD for reasons other than mere brevity, as we shall see) than with the form's function in and for television itself. For in order to begin to understand DD it is necessary to stand back from backbench and tabloid shock horror about the latest examples of the form and to look at it in its historical and institutional context. Indeed, only by analysing it as an integral – rather than in some sense exceptional – part of the history of British broadcasting can we hope to account for its continuing existence and occasionally controversial status. That status marks DD out as the most institutionally potent but at the same time problematic of the small screen's programme categories – the television equivalent of what, in film studies, are called genres (whose characteristics are usually as clear to consumers as they are to producers). In fact, so problematic is the designation DD that one needs to ask whether it is a programme category at all or simply a label attached to the most controversial programmes.

The politicians themselves, however, seem to be in no doubt about the form's identity as an easily distinguished species (which is ironic when one considers that one of the most familiar criticisms of DD is that viewers are unable to distinguish between it and documentary 'proper'). In 1980, when *Death of a Princess* was accused of igniting the worst international incident since Suez (the real 1956 event not the 1979 DD of the same name), Lord Carrington remarked that 'The new formula of mixing fact with fiction, dramatisation masquerading as documentary, can be dangerous and misleading.' Sir Ian Gilmour went further still by suggesting that 'the whole genre is something the IBA and BBC should give considerable attention to. . . . I think the so-called dramatisation or fictionalising of alleged facts or history is extremely dangerous and misleading.' Lord Carrington's description of DD as a 'new formula' is a useful place for this essay to start. After asking whether DD is, in fact, either a formula or new I will sketch out a skeletal history of the form in British television, follow it with an account of some of the definitions of and debates about it, and try finally and very briefly to relate it to the dominance of the realist aesthetic (and ideology) in British culture in general and the audio-visual media in particular.


## A new formula

Today television programme departments are so specialized that one could be forgiven for assuming that drama departments produce dramas, documentary departments produce documentaries, and so on. A truism, perhaps, but one that implies that in the absence of drama and documentary departments, and thus of co-productions between them, the hybrid of DD would never have been conceived. In fact, however, individual episodes of science programmes like *Horizon*, current affairs series like *This Week* and *Panorama*, arts strands like *Monitor* and *The South Bank Show*, and one-off drama slots like *The Wednesday Play* (not to mention entire crime series like *Z Cars* and soap operas like *Emergency Ward Ten*) have all been confidently categorized as DD in their time.

Furthermore, they have been so categorized not simply by critics or programme makers but by the very broadcasting authorities which Gilmour urges to consider the form. This is not to suggest that only an official institutional christening can legitimate the inclusion of any particular programme in the category. Rather, as the rest of this chapter will argue, many of the arguments about and allegations against DD have been mobilized very selectively and often very crudely against programmes with a clear-cut and avowedly oppositional politics. In this crucial sense DD is not a universal or ahistorical programme category, but a historically specific controversy about such categories; not so much a distinct genre as a debate about genre distinctions.

That the gentlemen's agreement about keeping the boundaries between fact and fiction on the small screen free from trespass is frequently broken can be no surprise to any regular viewer of reconstructions on the News or *Crimewatch* or of the latest costume drama. What may be more of a revelation to the ordinary viewer is that Lord Carrington's conviction that the formula is 'new' couldn't be further from the truth. DD is as old as television itself – the very definitions themselves were already in use long before the mid-1960s when the form first hit the headlines. DD is one of the oldest, if not the very oldest, narrative mode in British television. *The Times*, for instance, published a piece entitled 'Birth of the dramatized documentary' as early as 1961, but earlier still work was well under way. In 1956 Caryl Doncaster contributed an essay on 'The story documentary' to a book about television in which she remarked that 'The dramatized story documentary is one of the few art forms pioneered by television'.[1] And in his history of the BBC's TV script unit Roger Wade noted that 'in 1950 . . . the main interest among producers was the development of documentary drama which well fulfilled the BBC's three part charter for information, education and entertainment'.[2] (I shall return to the relationship between British television's historic public service obligations and the evolution of the DD towards the end of this chapter.) In fact Robert Barr, for one, was writing and producing so-called 'story documentaries' from 1946.

If the genre has been with us for some four decades why do so many politicians, programme makers and professional critics continue to talk as if it is 'new'? There are several possible answers to this question. Of course it is far easier to discredit something as aberrant if one can call it exceptional, literally unprecedented. And in the context of recent British politics – in which a postwar British consensus has apparently and irresolvably broken down – such aberrance has very rapidly become almost unforgivable. But a more general answer to the question is perhaps the simplest one of all: there is a widespread ignorance about television history in this country which those who make their living from the medium are often as guilty of as anyone.

## Developments in drama documentary

Before television, of course, the documentary reconstruction had a long and respectable pedigree in the cinema going back to Melies through figures as distinct as Eisenstein and Griffith and movements as diverse as neorealism and *cinéma-vérité*. And some historians of the form are tempted to trace its precursors back to Shakespeare's history plays and beyond. The British documentary film movement of the 1930s associated with John Grierson is perhaps the most important precedent here. It was Grierson who had first used the word documentary in 1936 in describing Robert Flaherty's film *Moana*. Grierson later defined documentary as 'the creative interpretation of reality'. One of Grierson's colleagues from documentary cinema, Paul Rotha, became the first head of the BBC's Television Documentary Department when it was set up in 1953.

In 1946 the BBC's postwar resumption of television transmissions had been marked, among other things, by the formation of a new unit, the Dramatized Documentary Group. Developing out of the BBC's obligation to document the new postwar Britain, the group was an outgrowth of the Illustrated Talks Department and was soon responsible for a large number of what the *Radio Times* described as 'story documentaries' with scripts, sets, and actors reconstructing (and thus 'documenting') an inaccessible world beyond the studio walls. The explanation for this was simple – in the era of live transmission the technology of television was simply too unwieldy to allow even the most rudimentary kind of documentary other than the outside broadcast of a 'major' national event. (An outside broadcast', or OB, tended to be restricted to pageants, sporting occasions, and so on.) Not until the advent of prerecording techniques in the form of videotape in the late 1950s or the introduction of more flexible, lightweight film equipment in the early 1960s could 'documentaries' (except the most expensive and prestigious ones) be other than 'dramatized'. Until then the making of a documentary on location meant extraordinarily cumbersome 35 mm cameras, huge cables, and heavy lighting equipment, all of which would have automatically precluded the kind of fluid and flexible observational style which would have been the only reason for leaving the studio in the first place. Take an example. If, in the second half of the 1940s a producer wanted to 'inform' her/his audience about career prospects in a particular industry, or, alternatively, about the social problems ordinary people encountered in specific areas of British life, there were only two alternatives. The first and most conventional was the illustrated talk: a doctor, lawyer, printer, or social worker would be invited to the studio to explain her/his work. The second way of representing this subject would be to 'recreate' it in the studio. Instead of bringing someone out of their natural/professional habitat to talk about it, some programme makers felt it was preferable to observe them at work (to do the research on location as it were) and then to try and recreate that experience in the studio. The BBC, after all, was keen to grasp the Griersonian nettle of 'explaining society to society' and so, week by week, dramatized documentaries on the courts, marriage, old age, delinquency, prostitution, industrial relations, and immigration were transmitted from the BBC studios. Robert Barr, who was responsible for the first programmes in this strand, started out by simply dramatizing 'How to' guides to the professions with titles like *I Want To Be An Actor* (1946) and *I Want To Be A Doctor*, but storylines soon became increasingly complex. The narrativization of public service – the placing of educational or informational content into entertaining form – was the origin of the so-called 'story documentary'.

In 1956 the BBC acquired Ealing Film Studios, partly in response to the documentary films already being made by the ITV companies (which, like ITN, had been able to equip themselves with newer, lighter cameras when they were set up in 1955) and partly in order to compete with the American film drama series which ITV was so successfully introducing to British screens. That year ITV also launched its anthology drama slot, *Armchair Theatre*, which was to prove so influential a forerunner of the BBC's own 'kitchen sink' school, and which shared many characteristics with the contemporary British cinema's new wave of films like *Saturday Night and Sunday Morning*. But as film recording became technically (and financially) more feasible for the nascent television documentary the live story documentary became increasingly anachronistic. In 1960 only two BBC drama documentaries were transmitted and in 1961 there was only one. But just as the imperative to dramatize technically inaccessible documentary subjects disappeared another category emerged, that of the original television drama deploying the devices and/or researches of the documentary to distinguish itself from adaptations of stage and page which had dominated television drama until then.

Formed in 1961, the Documentary Drama Group was as prolific as its predecessor and as avowedly populist. One of its first productions was a four-part series about crime called *Jacks and Knaves*, written by Colin Morris and directed by Gilchrist Calder. Calder and Morris were interviewed in *The Times* in 1961 in honour of 'The birth of the dramatised documentary', and *Jacks and Knaves* proved such a success that it functioned as a sort of pilot for the launch, early the next year, of *Z Cars*. The latter is an excellent example of the shifting 'form' as well as 'content' of television drama at the time. It was mostly shot on film with studio inserts and made much use of authentic locations like streets, pubs, factories, and so forth in stark contrast to the studio halls and corridors of live drama. And in terms of content it was also a departure – albeit one which with 25 years' hindsight looks rather formulaic. For it featured not an avuncular London bobby like Dixon in a cosy almost entirely uncriminal community, but four young policemen in a northern newtown precinct patrolling in the new panda cars (Z Victor One and Z Victor Two) – a Scotsman, a Welshman, an Englishman, and an Irishman. In every sense this precinct was a long way from Dock Green and the protagonists had both personal and professional problems of their own. This, as the critics noted at the time, was a new television realism. Realism, of course, being a relative term.

Meanwhile ITV was itself responsible for a group of series and serials which were being hailed as major in the area of DD: from *Emergency Ward Ten* and *Coronation Street* (both of which would be classified today as soap operas) to *Police Surgeon* and *Probation Officer* (which were closer to slightly off-beat crime series – the former was actually the prequel to *The Avengers*). It is crucial not to perceive this classification as some kind of anachronism or aberration. There are in fact several very good reasons why 1960s critics and audiences – as well as the broadcasting authorities themselves – should thus identify such programmes. For one thing they were regional dramas in ways which the bulk of previous series, serials, and single plays were not. ITV's federal structure and the ITA guidelines obliged the companies to document and dramatize the lives of those in their own localities regularly, and such programmes attempted to do just that. Furthermore, serials like *Coronation Street* seemed to be ushering onto the screen a social class (and a region and accent) hitherto all but unseen on the small screen.[3]

In 1962 as the BBC's Documentary Drama Group launched *Z Cars* another BBC department was celebrating the 100th edition of its prestigious arts anthology, *Monitor*. *Monitor* had not entirely outgrown its origins in the illustrated talk, often relying exclusively on the testimony of an actual artist who came into the studio to be interviewed about her/his work; alternatively a critic would be employed to guide the viewer through the work of a dead or otherwise unavailable painter or poet. But Ken Russell's dramatized documentary film about Edward Elgar in 1962

79

was to signal an entirely new departure in arts programming. The constraints of 'good television' (and good taste) and the conventions of arts programmes were such that Russell was refused permission to include dialogue scenes for the actors he had cast as Elgar and his wife, and a voiceover narration was added chronicling the composer's life in the conventional arts profile manner, but nevertheless the damage was done; a new subgenre, the arts feature dramatization, was born. Russell went on to experiment further with the forms and the results included *The Debussy Film*, *Song of Summer*, and *The Dance of the Seven Veils* – all for the BBC. Today something like LWT's *The South Bank Show* still retains the interview/profile of the artist format, whilst occasionally 'dramatizing' sequences from the interviewee's 'work' or 'life'.

In 1964 another breakthrough occurred. A young film maker working in the BBC's Talks Division documentary section made a film called *Culloden* about the 1745 Jacobite uprising of that name. But instead of treating this subject in the conventional manner with a barrage of maps and an exhibition of period relics on display in the studio to be disinterred by a presenter/historian, *Culloden*'s director Peter Watkins reconstructed the battle itself with an amateur cast and then filmed it in newsreel style with a lightweight 16 mm hand-held camera and an off-screen narrator/reporter. (Where Russell had to fight to get actors into his *Monitor* profiles Watkins had cleverly circumvented the same constraint by employing amateurs; soon enough, however, he was having to do battle with Equity to keep professional actors out of his work.) The following year Watkins was to apply this same 'documentary' style to the dramatization of an equally inaccessible event, this time set not in the remote past but in an all too imminent future. *The War Game* wasn't a reconstruction of an actual battle but a documentary-style prediction or 'preconstruction' of what the aftermath of a full scale nuclear attack would look like. *The War Game* was considered unshowable and was not transmitted until 1985.

1964 also saw the launch of the BBC's new single drama slot, *The Wednesday Play*, which was to be regularly associated with naturalistic depictions of social problems, particularly in the work of the producer Tony Garnett and the director Ken Loach. Plays like *Up the Junction* in 1965, *Cathy Come Home* in 1966, and *In Two Minds* in 1967 (which dealt with abortion, homelessness, and schizophrenia respectively) had an extraordinary impact both on British life in general (*Cathy Come Home* has been credited with the successful launch of the charity Shelter) and on the rest of British television. They mixed the techniques of drama, interview, newsreel, *nouvelle vague*, and so on but, perhaps most important, got out of the studio and onto the streets. And this, of course, meant yet another departure: television programming was no longer live, nor was it necessary to be constrained by videotape (though an Equity agreement ensured that around 10 per cent of every drama was electronically recorded in the studio). *In Two Minds*, it seems, was the first single drama on British television to escape this constriction (though Loach had previously got around it by telerecording the video sequences on film and then editing them along with the rest of his material on celluloid in the cutting room). And the existence of 16 mm film meant quite simply that another alibi for the making of DD – the technical obstacles which prohibited the documenting of reality outside the studio (except on major occasions) – could no longer apply. From now on the trend towards naturalism or documentary drama was a result not of a constraining technology but of a flexible one. BBC crews, for the first time in TV drama, were able to get into working-class streets, onto factory floors, and into housing estates – into those very places, in fact, where, as *The Wednesday Play*'s Sydney Newman pointed out, the people who watched television mostly lived and worked.

While *Play for Today*, which was launched in 1970 to replace *The Wednesday Play*, continued the DD tradition irregularly with titles like *Scum, Rank and File, The Spongers, United Kingdom*, and *The Legion Hall Bombing*, the early 1970s also saw the initiation of what critic John Caughie refers to as the drama documentary strand of the genre. Where what Caughie calls the BBC's documentary drama derived from the single play, Granada's dramatized documentaries or dramatized journalism emerged from non-fiction; they were a development of the work done by that company's current affairs department. Granada, which had rejected Peter Watkins' early film *Forgotten Faces* (about Hungary in 1956) had set up a weekly current affairs series called *World in Action* in 1963. The very first edition of that series had included a 'dramatized' confrontation between actors playing Kennedy and Khruschev. Other 'reconstructed' sequences followed, but it was not until 1970 that the *World in Action* team produced an entire edition thus dramatized. This *World in Action* 'special' was entitled *The Man Who Wouldn't Keep Quiet*. Leslie Woodhead, its producer-director, has described it as the film which launched 'a group of programmes . . . which have sought the aid of drama for a drama-documentary purpose'.[4] It was based on the diary of a Soviet dissident, Grigorenko, which had been smuggled out of the psychiatric prison where he was being held and, according to Woodhead, its contents were then scrupulously authenticated against such independent sources as were available.

This film set the mould for future Granada drama documentaries in several ways. First of all it was shot at Broadstone House, a half-empty mill in Stockport that has since served as a set for Prague, Poland, and Peking. Indeed, all of Granada's drama documentaries to date have been about either eastern Europe or revolutionary China, while all of the BBC *Wednesday Plays* and *Plays for Today* which could be called documentary dramas have been set in Britain. Where the imperative for 'dramatization' in the pioneer days of live television had been technological inaccessibility, the *raison d'être* for Granada's output in the genre was a kind of 'reporter' inaccessibility – the 'iron curtain'. (Similarly the single play strand of the genre could also claim a kind of inaccessibility clause in its defence here. *Law and Order*, for instance, was so critical of the legal institutions of this country that the Prison Officer's Association banned the BBC from filming inside their establishments for twelve months after its transmission; had it been a straight documentary it might not have been granted access in the first place. As in the days of live 'story documentaries' in the studio, DD actually offered its makers greater freedom to comment than a straight observational documentary would have done.) In 1977 Granada institutionalized these productions by setting up its own drama documentary unit. More than ten years later the concern about 'balance' and its obverse 'bias' is being extended noisily by the political Right towards drama in the form both of 'realist' popular series like *EastEnders* and *Casualty* and of controversial/naturalistic single plays and serials like *The Monocled Mutineer*. The latter was attacked in 1986 for its alleged historical inaccuracy and defended by the BBC's Bill Cotton as representing 'the greater truth' about the First World War. This exchange merely served to produce further confusion as to the relation between realism and truth. By the late 1980s the imperative toward dramatizing otherwise 'inaccessible' subjects was apparently being blocked by an increasingly abrasive political climate.

If the 1970s saw the beginnings of a shift away from the 'naturalistic' 'kitchen sink' school which some critics had associated with *The Wednesday Play* and a simultaneous trend away from one-off drama and towards series and serials as the BBC's belt was tightened, Granada (along with other dramatically inclined documentary makers) was actually being moved towards rather than away from DD by more or less the same economic imperatives. The explanation for this apparent contradiction is relatively simple. As soon as television drama was both all-film and made in colour it quite swiftly became much more of an economic commodity than it had ever been in the days of live transmission and film and tape hybrids. Furthermore, as the conservative political climate in general and the TV ratings battle in particular prompted documentaries to be more popular, there were trends towards serialization (away from one-offs) and the spread of biopics, costume drama, and sagas about royal and not-so-royal 'real' historical families. Of course, the very process of 'realist' dramatization encourages the personalization of politics and the narrativization of history.

The 1970s and 1980s also saw non-fiction series like *Horizon* and *Panorama* dipping their toes in the waters of DD. In 1980, in fact, a new drama documentary unit was set up inside the Science and Features Department at the BBC and this was soon busy producing serials like *The Voyage of Charles Darwin* and *Oppenheimer* (both of them, significantly, international co-productions, both of them with international subjects, both of them in a sense biopics). It is interesting to note that Peter Goodchild, who moved from *Horizon* to become producer of *Oppenheimer*, later became Head of Single Plays, directly responsible for *Screen Two*, the successor slot to *Play for Today*. Ironically, Goodchild's opposite number at Channel 4 and the man responsible for the *Film on Four* strand is David Rose who started out as an assistant on story documentaries at the BBC in the 1950s followed by a stint on *Z Cars* and, later on *Play for Today*. Both *Screen Two* and *Films on Four* still have their share of naturalistic film fiction – as does British cinema itself.

## Definitions

John Caughie's distinction between 'drama documentary' and 'documentary drama' is a useful one. (The abbreviations 'dramadoc' and 'docudrama' and the term 'faction', however, are essentially American usages and will not be employed here. On the other hand terms like 'story documentary' and 'dramatized documentary' are very much part of the tradition of British television.) Essentially Caughie's distinction is that drama documentary (or dramatized documentary) borrows its 'documentariness' from its content, from its basis in the lives and situations of real people – and from the professional pedigree of the programme makers themselves, like those at Granada. Documentary drama, on the other hand, takes its 'documentariness' from its form or style, which is often associated with the visual rhetoric of *cinéma-vérité* or a concealed investigatory camera. In Documentary Drama, therefore, the camera often gives the impression of being 'surprised' by the action. Other examples of the documentary drama 'style' include improvisational acting, gritty, grainy, unglamorous lighting, and a rough, raw sound quality.

Whatever our doubts about the rigorousness of these terms, though, they are hardly any more debatable than the broadcasters' own classifications of such familiar forms as crime series or soap operas. Granada, for instance, still refuses to concede that *Coronation Street* is a soap opera and indeed the ITA (the Independent Television Authority which was the precursor of today's IBA or Independent Broadcasting Authority) described the serial as a 'documentary drama' in its annual report in 1961. Similarly, when the BBC first began to produce crime series in the 1950s its Drama Department refused to have anything to do with them – *Dixon of Dock Green*, for instance, was made by the corporation's Light Entertainment department, as was the BBC's first soap opera, *The Grove Family*. *Z Cars*, on the other hand, was the first series to be made by the BBC's brand new Documentary Drama Group.

The Documentary Drama Group, set up in 1961, and the ITA's acknowledgement of ITV's own 'documentary drama' output that same year, were neither unique nor shortlived examples of the institutionalization of this controversial programme category. That neither the BBC nor the IBA would today classify either *Z Cars* or *Coronation Street* in the same way is not a sign of their past or present misunderstanding of the term but is rather evidence of the flexibility of the terms themselves. For the definition only applies when the reality status of any particular programme is open to question, not just aesthetically but also ethically or politically. And that, of course, is where the context of any programme comes in. One such context is obviously the political one in which programmes are made and shown and seen. But at least of equal importance is what might be called the television context of any such programme – not just its place in any night's or week's schedule but also its use or abuse of the conventions expected of it at the time of its transmission. This is what is meant by the reality status of any programme – a 'reality' relative to the programmes that have previously passed as 'realistic' in the same area.

That television has conventions, an aesthetic if you like, and thus a history as a form as well as a forum, is easily and conveniently forgotten. And this relates to two factors: first its massive popularity and extremely low cultural status; and second its avowedly realist aesthetic. The cliché of clichés about television is that it is a window on the world (that phrase was once the subtitle of *Panorama*); the medium is seen as a mirror, as transparent, reflective, neutral. It is of course none of these things. But it is the unproblematic assent to this idea of transparency, not just as an inherent condition of the medium but also as an essential, an ideal one, that leads people like those at Granada to feel so strongly about the ethics

84

of what they are doing. Leslie Woodhead, for instance, has even suggested that every programme should be prefaced by some sort of 'indication of the kind of credibility [it] would claim'. For Woodhead, the absence of such signposting threatens 'the implied contract between broadcasters and audience' and, worse still, 'risks prejudicing the credibility of other areas of factual programming'. This is an ingenious but disingenuous defence of his favoured variant of the genre. But elsewhere Woodhead has hinted that the hard and fast distinction between 'fact' and 'fiction', 'drama' and 'documentary', is itself a dubious one.

> In making any television programme, including documentary, the nature of the exercise is selectivity. What you have to work from is structureless and messy – you intervene in that and make something with shape. And of course it's an artifice – just like *The Nine O'Clock News* or *Tom and Jerry*.[5]

If DD is likely ever to prejudice the credibility of other areas of television – particularly the most authoritative ones – it is a powderkeg indeed.

The instrumental view of television – as no more than a window on the world – has for too long impelled television drama toward a realist aesthetic and contained documentary within an unreflective, unreflexive form. The critical consensus of the reviewer and the politician shares this refusal to recognize the 'structured', 'selective', 'artificial' character of both drama and documentary, fiction and non-fiction. And yet this very same instrumental view, together with the ideology of public service in British broadcasting, has been perhaps the most powerful motive and motor for the quantity, quality, and centrality of drama documentary and documentary drama to British television. If this is the case then it is perhaps arguable that the most provocative and polemical programmes in this genre are those which deconstruct the programme-making process – and thus the instrumental ideology which underpins it.

Let me give some examples. Ken Russell's *The Debussy Film*, made for the BBC in 1965, counterpoints the by now familiar Russell technique of actors personifying the artists and their entourage with a framing story about the making of a television film about Debussy. Ten years later Thames Television's weekly current affairs shows, *This Week*, transmitted an edition which did much the same job as Russell's film – or indeed as Watkins' *Culloden*. *This Week: 1844* was an attempt to answer the question: Had television been invented in 1844 how would a current affairs programme have covered the long and bitter coal strike in Northumberland and County Durham that spring? Like Watkins' use of

Michael Aspel's off-screen voice in *The War Game*, Thames' on-the-spot reporter was the familiar *This Week* regular Michael Hargreaves – though in this case in nineteenth-century costume. Both *The War Game* and *This Week: 1844*, therefore, employed familiar presenters to authorize their fictions; but at the same time the use of that device could be said to reveal the role which the voiceover conventionally performs in masking the artifice of everyday news and current affairs. *This Week: 1844* attempted to outrage viewers by its wilfully superficial – and anachronistic – treatment of the strike, a treatment which reflects attitudes (to strikes and to television) which are no longer consensual. It would be an interesting exercise to compare the treatments of strikes in the BBC's story documentary *Strike* (1955), *The Wednesday Play*, *The Big Flame* (1969), *This Week: 1844* (1976), and the Granada unit's *Strike* about the birth of Solidarity (1981).

This is not the place to discuss the relative success or failure of such programmes but it does belatedly raise the crucial question of the audience – that constantly referred to but never adequately addressed aspect of the whole debate. (One key programme, *The Cheviot, The Stag and the Black, Black Oil*, even included its own audience by mixing the recording of a stage performance with film sequences both dramatized and documentary.) The assumption that the form is somehow a misleading one has all kinds of patronizing implications, since the complaining critic is clearly not among those so misled and yet can somehow sense the dangers of the form and reveal them for the benefit of his or her more vulnerable fellow viewers. Ironically the foregoing sketch of the form and the accompanying analysis of attitudes to it (exemplified by the reactions of those conservative politicians quoted earlier) reveal that both, in different ways, owe their origins to the paternal characteristics of public service broadcasting in this country.

*Death of a Princess* is also, in a sense, a deconstruction of the documentary form, and one which reveals the extent to which documentary film makers are themselves often veiled. Thus instead of simply reconstructing the story of the execution of a Saudi princess – the incident which inspired the film – director Antony Thomas' protagonist is not the princess but the documentary director wishing to make a film about her. And what emerges is a portrait of documentary film-making as bound by custom and practice, by the ideologies of objectivity, professionalism, and balance – all of which are surrounded by an almost metaphysical mystique; by values which are at least as suspect as those which the naive protagonist at first thought he was discerning among the Saudis. In spite of the international incident that ensued, the power of

Thomas' film is less its image of the execution of a princess than its more subtle assassination of the idea of documentary itself, the very conviction that drama and documentary are in some sense 'natural', 'neutral', and mutually exclusive categories rather than constantly fought-out frontiers within the cultural institutions of broadcasting.

## Notes

1 Caryl Doncaster, 'The story documentary', in Paul Rotha (ed.), *Television in the Making*, London: Focal Press, 1956.
2 Roger Wade, *Where the Difference Began*, London: BBC Script Unit, 1975.
3 See Richard Dyer (ed.), *Coronation Street*, London: British Film Institute, 1981.
4 Leslie Woodhead, 'A strike with a difference', in *Three Days in Szczecin*, Manchester: Granada Television, 1976. Reprinted in Goodwin, Kerr, and Macdonald, op. cit. in Further reading, p. 25.
5 Leslie Woodhead interviewed by John Wyver in 'Invasion', *Time Out*, 15–21 August 1980. Reprinted in Goodwin, Kerr, and Macdonald, op. cit. in Further reading, p. 32.

## Further reading

Caughie, John, 'Progressive television and documentary drama', *Screen*, vol. 21, no. 3 (1980).
Goodwin, A., Kerr, P., and Macdonald, I. (eds), *Drama-Documentary*, BFI Dossier no. 19, London: British Film Institute, 1983.
Kerr, P., 'A response to Caughie', *Screen*, vol. 22, no. 1 (1981).

# 6 BOX POP: POPULAR TELEVISION AND HEGEMONY

*Michael O'Shaughnessy*

After the tensions and anxieties of everyday life, people welcome the opportunity to sit down, relax and be made to smile and laugh. (*IBA Handbook* 1978)

If your life is unsatisfactory, there's always a new shampoo to try, a new Spielberg movie to see, the next instalment of a TV sit-com, the chance of winning a lottery. (Robin Wood)[1]

In the last few years there has been much study of 'popular culture', an area in which television programmes are perceived as a central concern. I want to look at how popular culture has been conceived as a broad context for thinking about the ideological meaning and pleasures of popular television programmes. So, what is 'popular culture', how has it been understood and why did cultural theorists become interested in it?

Popular culture is difficult to define because of its diversity; football, Christmas celebrations, Space Invaders, bingo, disco dancing, *EastEnders*, MacDonalds, and fish and chips might all be included. Yet there are common defining characteristics; first, for my purposes, popular culture refers to those activities and pastimes which take place outside the constraints of work as a part of *leisure* time, and which are perceived by consumers as providing forms of *pleasure* and *entertainment*. Second, 'popular' combines two meanings: originally 'popular' culture referred to

the culture 'of the people', to folk and working-class cultural pursuits produced for the people and by the people. From some leftwing perspectives this has been seen as the only authentic and politically correct form of culture.[2] With the developing technology of the twentieth century this culture has been disappearing fast, and the second meaning of 'popular' refers to those cultural forms which, through the rapid and easy dissemination of the mass media, are consumed by large numbers of people.

This culture is produced *for* the people *by* small groups who own and control the communications apparatus of the mass media (it has often been disparagingly labelled 'mass culture'). In our definition 'popular culture' includes both elements: it is produced through a combination and intersection of the mass-media technology controlled by socially dominant groups, and the interests and culture of the people who use and consume these. So, 'popular cultural' forms are produced by mass-production techniques yet at the same time are genuinely 'of the people' in their usage.

Why have academics, critics, and cultural theorists become interested in 'popular culture'? The interest first came from those who saw how much time, money, and energy went into 'popular culture's' production and consumption and who felt that mass-media products were aesthetically inferior and morally harmful. Attention was paid to 'popular culture' in order to protect people from it through a form of 'innoculation' (see below).

The second wave of interest has a socialist perspective based around the Marxist theories of 'ideology' and 'hegemony'. Both these concepts are used as a way of understanding how the dominant groups of any society maintain and retain their power over subordinate groups (women, ethnic minorities, the working class, and so on). Whereas earlier Marxist theories stressed the economic and material conditions of life as crucial determining factors, these concepts stress the importance of the way people think and feel – their commonsense consciousness or ideology – for maintaining the power and hegemony of the dominant groups and for obtaining the consent of the people to their own subordination. This *consciousness* can be understood as the ways in which we 'make sense' of the world, giving some kind of coherence to the society around us.

'Ideology' is rather a functional term: it seems to suggest that a dominant ideology or way of 'making sense' of the world is produced by the dominant groups and then dispensed to the rest of the population who simply lap it up. 'Hegemony' recognizes the role of the subordinate groups in producing ways of 'making sense' of the world. It suggests that the 'hegemony' or power of the dominant groups can only be maintained through a struggle and tension between dominant and subordinate groups. Out of this struggle, ways of 'making sense' of the world are produced which both groups contribute to and can agree with. What this means is that although the interests of the two groups are fundamentally opposed they have found a way of living in harmony or consent because the subordinate groups have won enough concessions to make them accept their domination while the dominant groups' overall structural power base is maintained. As long as *this* is not challenged the subordinate groups can continue to win more and more concessions and have an effect on the constitution of the resulting state of hegemony. So, in the establishment and negotiations of the hegemony of the dominant groups there is a struggle between the contradictory desires of all groups which finds areas of consent and consensus.

All this may seem a little complex but it provides a framework for thinking about 'popular culture', for helping us to understand such phenomena as popular involvement in the royal weddings, the World Cup, Live Aid, and the popularity of *EastEnders*, Madonna, Boy George, and *That's Life*. For 'popular culture' has its own ways of 'making sense' of the world; it offers us ways of understanding our society and thus contributes to the consciousness we have of the world; the argument of the cultural critics is that because of its stress on pleasure and entertainment it addresses everyone across class, age, gender, and thus becomes one of the most crucial sites in which our 'consciousness' is constructed, through which ideologies are produced, and by which hegemony is established. The popular press, pop music, popular television, and all forms of popular entertainment are central agencies for this process. Once the concerns of ideology and hegemony are realized we can never again see 'popular culture' as 'just entertainment' and socially insignificant.

In contributing to the establishment of hegemony 'popular culture' does contradictory things: it wins the support of the people while maintaining the power of the dominant groups and the oppression of the people. *Herein lies the fascination and central contradiction of 'popular culture' and television in their ability to do both these things at once, gratifying the people yet contributing to their enslavement.* The issues for us are to see *how* it does this and to ask if it always acts in this way or whether sometimes 'popular culture' can challenge the *status quo* of domination.

I have in a way begun to answer my third question – how has 'popular culture' been understood? Crudely it has been seen in two contradictory lights which partly answer the above ideological questions. The negative view sees it as the new 'opiate of the people' which keeps the masses moronically content with their lot and their oppression. The positive, as a form of the people's own cultural values, separate from and more authentic than the 'high' culture of the middle classes, and which can be a means of challenging the *status quo*. Historically we can see that at certain moments one or other of these positions may be more in evidence; for example the positive view is manifest in the strong radical press of the mid-nineteenth century or the popular postwar reconstruction period, while the negative may be found in descriptions of the late-Victorian music hall, described as a 'culture of consolation',[3] or the Hollywood escapist films of the 1930s Depression which caused Hollywood to be described as a dream factory. Obviously neither position offers the 'correct' answer, but the two provide a framework for the analysis of particular cases and point us towards my argument that popular culture in general and television in particular are contradictory sites.

These contradictory trends of thought do not only come from a leftwing perspective; they are shared by other intellectual traditions. One of the reasons we might find it difficult to assess 'popular culture' is that these positions are so deeply rooted in our culture that they have become embedded in our commonsense and unconscious ways of thinking about the world. Ask yourself the question: 'What do I think of *Crossroads*, *The Price is Right*, *Blind Date* or *Minder*?' Try listening to any group of people discussing last night's viewing. Many of us will dismiss such television in one breath as 'trash', 'rubbish', or 'trivia', and, in the next, rave about the latest episode of *Auf Wiedersehn, Pet* or ask intently what's happened now to Den and Angie of *EastEnders*. Students in discussion will often deny that they ever even watch such programmes, preferring news, current affairs, and serious drama, but moments later admit to their intimate familiarity with Terry Wogan and Les Dawson. The more honest may admit to their enjoyment but preface this by saying: 'I know I shouldn't like these programmes . . .'. We should note this desire to deny the validity of our own pleasures in popular cultural forms. I want to trace some of the intellectual traditions from which these contradictory 'gut' feelings derive.

Richard Dyer[4] has shown how contradictory views about 'entertainment' go back in two traditions to the seventeenth-century French philosophers Pascal and Montaigne. Both traditions see entertainment as easy, pleasurable, hedonistic and democratic as opposed to the serious, refined and cognitively difficult nature of an elitist 'high' culture; both see entertainment offering available pleasures *in the face of the problems of life*. The tradition following from Pascal sees this form of entertainment as an escape which is ultimately self-destructive since it is merely a way of reconciling us to the *status quo*, of making us accept the conditions of life as it is – so that, for example, the pleasures of drinking, dancing, sport, TV, and sex carefully structured into our weekends become the fodder which sustains and reproduces us as workers so that we will carry on with our drudgery for another week. The tradition deriving from Montaigne suggests that the escape of entertainment does more than make us cope with life, it actually leads us to question and criticize the *status quo* by reference to an ideal world, while also filling us with positive vitality. The utopia of entertainment is not an escapist illusion but an ideal to be strived and hoped for. In Dyer's words, then, the field of entertainment can be seen as 'a battleground' between these opposing tendencies.

The assertion, since the 1960s, of the second tradition, brought a breath of fresh air to cultural politics which tended to validate the possibilities of popular culture and entertainment, but there have also been two schools of thought in the twentieth century endorsing the negative view. The first sprang from a rightwing perspective, valuing the 'difficult' works of high culture, and from which popular culture was a problem on two levels. *Morally*, popular culture was a subversive form which threatened to corrupt people, particularly the young, and was dangerously anti-social: cheap thrills and pleasures could undermine the values of society. Since the war this view has had a particularly anti-American stance. Given the democratic nature of popular culture this fear is actually well-founded.[5] The argument was reinforced by *aesthetic* judgements which saw popular culture as inferior. The approach of conservative educationalists once they realized the influence popular culture was beginning to have on teenagers was the 'innoculation' approach: by analysing a little popular culture you taught people to recognize and discriminate against its shoddiness and thus reject it. We might suspect that a contradiction was already in play for those teachers studying things they really enjoyed only to morally pat themselves on the back, saying that they now knew why these things were so 'rotten'. Such views are found in a British cultural analytical tradition from Matthew Arnold to F. R. Leavis.

The other school of thought endorsing the negative view of popular culture came from those socialist critics of the Frankfurt School, mostly German *émigrés*, who went to America in the 1930s to escape the Nazis. They attempted to understand the relation between culture and fascism and they made a distinction between high art and popular culture: popular culture was the opiate helping to maintain the *status quo* of a conservative society; high art was the realm in which it was possible to challenge society. Indeed high art, if it was any good, was *always* critical of society.

According to Marcuse, 'Art is the Great Refusal – the protest against that which is'. The artist's function was to provide a negative critique of society since 'the higher culture was always in contradiction with social reality'.[6] Popular mass art offered escapist wish-fulfilments, providing comfort or excitement which would 'serve as instruments of social cohesion'. The media thus become instruments of manipulation and indoctrination. The Frankfurt School also recognized the socio-economic context of the production and consumption of cultural products; they coined the term 'culture industry'. They argued that *all* cultural products within the capitalist market simply became commodities for consumption. As commodities they would all be reduced to the same value so that even 'high' oppositional art could now be marketed and contained, thus losing its challenging meanings.

There are problems with the Frankfurt School's approach: an elitism which devalues popular and working-class forms, denying their oppositional possibilities, a suspicion of pleasure, and an assumption of a passive audience which will simply soak up whatever is offered. But they did open up a serious ideological understanding of the role of popular culture. Today, many radicals take a different view; we believe that any serious and lasting social changes can only be carried through by changes in popular consciousness. Popular culture is more significant than high, elitist culture in producing consciousness, and therefore it is in this area that socialists must seek oppositional work. Popular culture needs to be re-evaluated ideologically and aesthetically. To accept its validity it is necessary to:

(i) overcome a cultural snobbishness about the values of easy art forms;
(ii) overcome a puritan heritage which wants to deny pleasure;
(iii) recognize the potential positive elements for popular culture to challenge the *status quo*.

However, we mustn't go overboard. While recognizing this site as politically crucial, we must remember that at the moment much, if not most, popular culture ultimately continues to serve the interests of the dominant groups. Understanding this may lead to attempts to change the current forms of popular culture.

Before turning to popular television there's one further piece of theory which may prove useful for analysis; this is the concept of 'incorporation' or 'containment'. The Frankfurt School saw the process of incorporation (literally being taken into the body of) as the way in which any radical or critical elements could be swallowed up, neutralized, and made safe by the culture industry, so that they lost their critical meanings. We can see a similar process of containment in the way that hegemony works. Since hegemony is produced through the interests of both dominant and subordinate groups, we can say that some challenging elements will be included within the hegemonic consent. But since the overall power structure remains intact these challenges are incorporated.

How do these general arguments look when applied to popular television? The opening of commercial television in 1955 saw the beginning of the BBC/ITV battle for audiences. The BBC had previously produced what it felt was 'good' for people. ITV, with a recipe of light entertainment, soap operas, and quiz shows like *Double Your Money* and *Take Your Pick*, changed all that. From now on audiences, through viewing choices, *did* have a say in what was produced, because TV had to win viewers. Yet television remained in the hands of a small, elite group of financiers, controllers, and programme makers whose broad interests were still those of the capitalist state. Here is generated the central contradiction of TV: the fact that it is 'a discourse generated "from above" which must nevertheless win consent, gain credibility and acceptance "from below".'[7]

In addition to this, some critics have noticed how the dominant groups' ideological and economic needs do not necessarily always correspond.[8] The ideological needs require TV programming which will help *reproduce* the existing relations of power; programmes function ideologically. Economic needs are just about profit: programmes are about winning audiences. What happens if popular programmes are ideologically unacceptable? It could be that commercial television, motivated by short-term economic needs, will be more radical in such situations than public service broadcasting, and economic power and needs would outweigh ideological ones. However, at present television for the most part seems to be holding together its twin aims of winning the support of a large audience while ideologically contributing to the maintenance of the dominant social groups' power.[9] How does it do these two things?

**Winning support**

Television must connect with people's actual experiences, both in terms of our real lives and our fantasy lives; unless we can recognize ourselves, our desires, and our dreams in television it will mean nothing to us. Television must be relevant and up to date; successful drama, based on conflict, is drawn to issues and problems of the moment. We can see how

94

situation comedies and soap operas constantly work over issues about the family and sexuality, how police/crime series are always dealing with social problems, 'deviancy', and questions about 'law'n'order'. Each new autumn series of programmes reflects the latest shift in the ground rules of everyday reality; for example, situation comedies which used to focus on the problems of the nuclear family are now dealing more and more with the problems of one-parent, divorced, unmarried, or 'deviant' families. The challenge to *Coronation Street* by *EastEnders* can also be seen as the triumph of a more up-to-date image of the world. The appeal of non-realist programmes like *Dallas* and *The Young Ones* is through their connection with our current fantasy desires. Even game shows like *Play Your Cards Right* use questions which deal with current concerns around sexual equality: 'We asked a hundred secretaries: "Could you do your boss's job as well as he does?" How many secretaries said they could?' The questions on this programme present a perfect example of hegemony in action as we see the referencing of socially accepted norms in the assumptions behind the questions – that the world is peopled by bosses and secretaries (male and female), but there is then a chance to show the inequality of this system since the secretaries reply that they see themselves as equally capable. The 'correct' and 'popular' answers to the questions are then negotiated in a struggle between Bruce Forsyth (the question master), the contestants, and the audience. But the initial questions already presuppose tensions and fractures in 'normal' social relations. So, to win support, programmes are drawn to difficult ideological areas which will then have to be negotiated.

Programmes also win support through offering us pleasures. These may be the pleasures of, first, heightened emotion: laughter at comedies, suspense with crime shows and snooker, emotional involvement and tears with soap operas; secondly, aural and visual spectacle: the video-generated effects of *Top of the Pops*, the coverage of sports events, the sexual spectacle of Benny Hill's Angels; thirdly, narrative: the weekly instalments in the serial, the culmination of the quiz show in the $64,000 question; fourthly, stars and identification figures: from Jimmy Hill to Ian McGaskill, from Terry Wogan to Wincey Willis; or, fifthly, familiarity: familiar faces and recurring theme tunes.

## Ideological work

The ideological/hegemonic operations of popular television are not simple, initially because many programmes, in the way they negotiate social issues, are themselves contradictory. They can include several different 'discourses'; they are open to various audience readings; they have to be seen in a wider social context. It is possible to argue for positive and negative readings of almost all popular television genres. Some comedies can be read as socially disruptive, subversive, and anarchic – The Young Ones and Spitting Image – or as a social safety valve for letting off steam for a moment which certainly won't change the world. (The first Spitting Image series was very close to being banned but by the third series having a Spitting Image puppet made of you was seen as a sign and confirmation of star status.) Game shows, like The Price is Right, can be celebrated as utopian representations of community, abundance, energy and people's participation or seen as sexist endorsement of capitalist consumerism and competitiveness in which contestants are totally manipulated. Are soap operas a setting for strong female characters, addressing female viewers with a feminine voice, or so rooted in the domestic trivia of life that any pertinent social comment is evacuated in the face of unrealistic and rosy representations of working-class communities? Programmes can include several sets of meanings. They contain several 'discourses' or points of view. When analysing Juliet Bravo are we concerned with the representations of law and order, of women, or of social problems? The series may be positive in showing how crime is caused by social problems like unemployment and bad housing, positive in showing a professionally capable woman, yet negative in showing the police as politically neutral and incorruptible. Which discourse are we concerned with? How do they combine? Which is most important? It may be that the positive elements win us as audience to accepting this view of the police. These are partly textual problems but they point us to questions about audiences and how they understand programmes (see chapter 4). Different audiences may make different and contradictory readings. These readings will also be affected by the contexts of programmes: an unusually provocative programme can be instantly incorporated by its positioning between adverts and Emmerdale Farm; its meaning is lost in the 'flow' of television which reduces it to a single element of the day's familiar and forgettable menu; the popular press coverage of EastEnders may have boosted audiences but it tends to favour a view of the programme as being about gossip and scandal rather than social criticism.

While I've emphasized some of the contradictions in the programmes there are ways in which they clearly do support the dominant groups because they do not challenge these groups' power. Ideology works by masking, displacing, and naturalizing social problems and contradictions. These processes can be seen in the form and content of television.

Television constructs a view of the world but *naturalizes* that view, makes it normal, by hiding its own means of construction, its editing, selection, and camerawork. It claims to offer a 'window on the world' as though its mediating processes were not there at all. Realism, TV's dominant dramatic form, operates in a similar fashion. Television assumes naturally given values in its 'mode of address', the way it speaks to us as viewers. Chapter 2 has referred to the way television constructs a 'family audience'. TV also constructs us as naturally patriotic British subjects whenever it covers sports or royal occasions: 'We'll all be rooting for England tonight.' 'Good news today as we celebrate the Queen's 60th birthday.' Our inclusion is natural and unproblematic.

*Masking* and *displacement* are more complex. They are the means by which social contradictions are hidden or diverted into other areas. Displacement occurs through omission; some problems and viewpoints are just not dealt with (for example, there is no coverage of many Irish issues). It also happens through the privileging of certain issues over others. Gender conflict is often foregrounded (in the *Play Your Cards Right* questions), but class and racial conflict are given less space. It occurs through 'mode of address': we are addressed as British families who are consumers interested in entertainment. This may be an accurate description but it's not the whole story; we could be addressed as workers or members of different classes, gender, and races. By focusing on categories which bind us together in unity, TV 'displaces' or hides our differences and potential social antagonisms.

The narrative forms of television and its use of genre can also mask social contradictions. Three aspects of narrative – the form itself, its stress on individuals, and the way it resolves problems – all contribute to this. First, we take pleasure in narrative from the form itself; the setting up of a mystery or problem which we know will be dramatically resolved. We can get more caught up in the process of narrative development than in what the story is actually about. Secondly, most narratives are about individuals we can identify or empathize with. The focus on individuals means we may lose sight of people as representations of social groups and therefore pay less attention to society and its institutions. Thirdly, as Raymond Williams has remarked, there are 'magical' endings to some stories, whereby complex problems are suddenly solved by a twist of fate or coincidence which will provide a happy ending. TV uses similar 'magical' endings as a way of dealing with the complex social problems it may have set up.

Narratives and their endings do not have to work like this. *Edge of Darkness* and *Dead Head* were much more uncompromising in their questionings, respectively, of the use of nuclear power and the controls of the state; they challenged some of the above conventions. But they can still be seen as incorporated in terms of form – 'Well that was an exciting story' – or TV flow – 'And next week sees the start of a brand new series.'

If narrative is limiting, what about genres? Popular television's output is centred around several types of programme or genres: soap operas, sitcoms, quiz shows, and so forth. There are sound economic reasons for this: the ease and economy of production, using the same sets, actors, producers, and the guarantee of an audience who will return to what has already been established as popular. (You could argue that all television operates on the level of generic series – even *The News* and *The Weather*.) There is also the principle of repetition and variation both in terms of series within the whole genre and plots and characters within particular series. *Minder* works within the framework of a three-act, 55-minute drama series concerned with crime in London (compare with *The Sweeney*, *The Gentle Touch*, and *The Bill*). Each week Arthur Daley and Terry appear; Arthur exploits Terry, Terry minds for Arthur; each week there is a new story with some new characters. Our pleasure is in the repetition of a known situation and its new developments. Who will the guest stars be? Will Terry get one up on Arthur this week? At the point when a particular generic series loses popularity a new brand will be introduced. (This is as true for game shows as fiction series.) Many radical TV writers recognize that generic series and serials are *the* medium to work in to win a popular audience and they believe that these forms have enormous progressive potential. But the dominance of genre programmes does present problems:

(i) The popularity of genres marginalizes those programmes which do not fit into generic conventions, since audiences will not recognize them.
(ii) As with narrative, generic form can predominate over content.
(iii) Generic structures can be ideologically limiting. The crime series tends to focus on policemen as familiar characters, automatically putting us on their side. The form of sit-com is to maintain an original situation week after week. It is formally bound to maintain the *status quo*. This means that though an interesting problem might be set up, the question of infidelity in *Butterflies* for example, it can never actually be answered and allow any progression.

There are some programmes which break with the conventions of the genre. *Hill Street Blues* crossed the crime/police genre with soap opera and sit-com; *The Young Ones* pushed the 'realist' situation of comedy to its limits. Programmes which break rules often build up cult audiences, offering us pleasures dependent on awareness of genre manipulation, but in a fairly short time even these programmes become conventionalized and normal. The progressive potentialities of genre may lie in introducing radical content in the way that *Brookside* has consciously attempted.

These last points raise questions of pleasure and ideology. Criticism of TV in the 1970s aimed to expose its ideological operations, but neglected pleasure. This is central in winning audiences (see above). There is no doubt that existing television companies are well placed in terms of money, equipment, and professional expertise to produce pleasurable programmes, and questions of pleasure will often outweigh ideological concerns for an audience (myself included). Any radical TV will only succeed if it too provides pleasure.

However, pleasures can be thought of ideologically. Much humour depends on a racist common sense, for example to 'get' Irish jokes. Enjoyment of TV spectacle often relies on treating women as objects of visual pleasure. Pleasure in narrative and generic forms can also be limiting (see above). Maybe we should think in terms of progressive and reactionary pleasures. Certainly Brecht believed in a form of popular enjoyment and 'pleasurable learning' where the pleasure was for exploited groups in understanding their oppression and how to challenge it. Brecht compared this with the reactionary pleasures of identification, excitement, and spectacle which he would see in much of today's TV. However, even these forms can't be totally condemned. As Dyer has argued, traditional forms of entertainment do offer radical possibilities in showing us utopian and ideal visions which allow an escape from the present but also implicitly criticize the present.

Let us take one final example of a programme which wins popular support. *That's Life* is a blend of light entertainment and serious 'watchdog' programme; it has run for more than ten years on BBC 1, mostly occupying a primetime Sunday evening viewing slot.

*That's Life* is interesting first because it is a programme which appears to offer the people their own voice. It is a form of access TV in which virtually all items derive from letters and calls from 'you the public', and in many of which the public actually appears. It can thus be seen as a programme 'of the people', though of course all items are framed and mediated by the professional TV team of Esther Rantzen and her colleagues. Secondly, the programme's 'watchdog' elements point to the problems, contradictions, and exploitations of today's capitalist, bureaucratic state. However, despite this, the programme's dominant position is one which wins support to acceptance of the *status quo*.

How does it do this? In dealing with the problems of daily British life, the programme constantly draws attention to the anomalies and exploitations within our system and state but it never questions the overall system itself. The 'people', generally positioned not in terms of class or work, but as consumers and/or family members, suffer at the hands of bureaucracy, small and big business, incompetence, bungling, and petty mindedness. Television is the impartial third estate, outside Parliament and the law, the instrument of free speech, the voice of the ordinary man and woman in the street. It focuses people's complaints and criticisms of various powerful groups within our society, but at the same time it never actually challenges the ground rules of a capitalist consumerist society, and ultimately it calls on the state institutions of Parliament and the law to reform institutions or punish offenders.

While part of the programme wins our support by attacking various power groups, another part shows the human and caring side of these same institutions. Regular features include various public bodies or private enterprise groups performing acts which put to rights earlier blunders. These are often framed as song and dance numbers or situation comedy sketches, within the discourse of light entertainment. For example, one local council group of civil servants respond to a letter from a couple about a tree that needs pruning. We see the various stages of bureaucracy needed to implement this action; the whole piece is put together in song to the tune of 'There'll Always Be An England', and the final chorus unites all levels of management and workers involved. Class hierarchies are shown, but unity, not conflict, is produced under the patriotic national sign of the Union Jack. The state is shown to be unified, caring, and responsive. But furthermore it is talented.

We are here brought back to the discourse of light entertainment. The utopian pleasures of light entertainment are generally non-antagonistic, and the discourse offers us, in Richard Dyer's words, abundance, energy, and community – TV presents us with a 'wonderful world'. This world, opposed to the 'real' world of conflict, is the world of television and entertainment itself. It is a world which is increasingly dwelt on in the popular press; it is a world of rewards, through actual appearance, consumer goods, or simply pleasure; it is a self-referential world in which understanding and pleasure presuppose great television knowledge. *That's Life* offers us, the public, the chance to enter this world; we can send in humorous and witty items or perhaps perform ourselves with our talented domestic pets or our own peculiar musical talents. The blending of ordinary people with the TV world is complete when the public perform with members of the *That's Life* team. Members of the team themselves have nowadays to be talented light entertainers as well as good 'watchdog' reporters. The discourse of light entertainment (which also suffuses the serious reports where narratives are often played for laughs) becomes the dominant discourse of the whole programme. (The end of a series highlights programme features, mainly entertainment items.) This is a discourse which is ultimately optimistic and positive, confirming that life is alright. This position is finally achieved in the common sense of the programme's title, *That's Life*. This phrase connotes an understanding of the unfairness of the world, of the crazy humour of the world, and of the eternal never-changing nature of the world that is life. At one and the same time it criticizes and accepts our world. This is a common sense which embodies and is full of contradictions. If we start to examine what 'life' is, the contradictions are apparent and uncomfortable. But *That's Life* is a phrase which cements things over; it is a final comment, one made to close things off in acceptance, rather than open them up. Yet this remains a programme which in its vox pop interviews allows the voice of an old black working-class woman to speak freely and for the audience to endorse Esther Rantzen's suggestion that this woman be the next prime minister. Is this the challenge or incorporation of alternative voices? It is a programme which 'makes sense' of our world, winning our acceptance of it through the discourses of common sense and light entertainment; but it also 'makes sense' by voicing, showing and trying to deal with our problems and contradictions.

## Notes

Thanks to Susan Boyd-Bowman for her comments and suggestions on this article.

1 Robin Wood, *From Hollywood to Vietnam*, New York: Columbia University Press, 1986.
2 See, for example, Richard Hoggart, *The Uses of Literacy*, London: Penguin, 1958.
3 Gareth Stedman Jones, 'Working-class culture and working-class politics in London 1870–1900: notes on the remaking of a working class', in Bernard Waites, Tony Bennett, and Graham Martin (eds), *Popular Culture: Past and Present*, London: Croom Helm, 1982.
4 R. Dyer, 'The social value of entertainment', unpublished PhD thesis, University of Birmingham, Centre for Contemporary Cultural Studies. See also his BFI Monograph *Light Entertainment*.
5 H. Marcuse, *One Dimensional Man*, London: Routledge & Kegan Paul, 1964.
6 ibid.
7 S. Hall, 'Cultural Studies: two paradigms' in *Media, Culture and Society*, vol. 2, no. 1, London: Academic Press, 1981.

8 R. Dyer T. Lovell, and J. McCrindle, 'Soap opera and women', *Edinburgh TV Festival Programme*, 1977.
9 During the 1960s and 1970s television was the most important of the mass media; it had replaced cinema as the major source of entertainment and information. However, it may be that in the 1980s we are witnessing another shift in which media technology as we have known it for the past 20 years is being challenged and altered by the appearance of a new channel, video, cable, satellite, and computers. TV may cease to win its mass support in the face of these rival entertainments unless it again transforms itself, as in the late 1950s, to ensure its continued popularity.

## Further reading

Bennett, Tony, *et al.* (eds), *Popular Television and Film*, London: British Film Institute, 1981.
Gurevitch, Michael, *et al.*, *Culture, Society and the Media*, London: Methuen, 1982.
Masterman, Len, *Television Mythologies*, London: Comedia, 1984.

# 7 WINNER TAKES ALL: COMPETITION

## Garry Whannel

Television has always offered a wide range of competition, from cricket to *Come Dancing*, from *Match of the Day* to *Mastermind*, from tennis to *Treasure Hunt*, from boxing to *Blankety Blank*. Fiske and Hartley[1] argue that, despite the obvious differences between these diverse forms of competition, they also have notable similarities. They all involve the ritualization and evaluation of social behaviour and all draw on the appeal of exploiting and resolving uncertainty. Characteristically, we are placed in the position of an evaluator or judge, able to sit back and assess performance.

Clearly this range of competitive forms on television is only part of a broader cultural passion for competition, as the extraordinary success of Trivial Pursuits shows. Competition on television both provides a structure for diverse forms of entertainment, and acts as the bearer of an overarching ideology about the importance of winning. But here it is necessary to be much more specific, and to pinpoint differences as well as similarities within the world of competition. Winning is important, but how important? What is won, what skills are necessary, and what are the costs of defeat?

There are clear distinctions to be made between quiz and game shows, and televised sport. Quiz and game shows depend on the display of knowledge or performance of skill, the acquisition of prizes, the display of celebrity and personality, all presented in terms of fun and games. Sport also depends on the performance of skill but, rather than fun and games, the emphasis lies on serious elite excellence. The spectacle and drama is intensified and the narrative question, 'who will win?', is foregrounded.

But as television sought to transform sport into a suitable form for television entertainment one by-product was a whole range of programmes that could be termed quasi-sport, blending elements of sport and light entertainment. *Superstars* and *Its a Knockout* are both examples of this tendency.

## Quiz and game shows

With the exception of the intellectual quizzes (*Mastermind*, *University Challenge*, and so on) few televisual forms have as low a cultural status as quiz shows. They are regularly derided by middle-class opinion, criticized in government reports, and restricted both in quantity and value of prizes by the IBA. Yet they are consistently popular (*Mastermind* included) and have the great advantage, for television, of being cheap to produce.

At first sight they would appear to be primarily about the display of knowledge, and the acquisition of prizes or status through the possession of and performance of particular sorts of knowledge. General knowledge questions have been a quiz show staple from *Double Your Money* and *Take Your Pick* to *The Krypton Factor* and *Fifteen to One*. The intellectual quizzes, *Mastermind* and *University Challenge* merely depend on a specialist variant of knowledge. But is is a very particular kind of knowledge, consisting of individual discrete facts. John Tulloch points out that quizzes feature isolated individuals under pressure, that they directly penalize thinking, give no room for interpretation, and celebrate knowledge as possession of facts, and argues that such a view of knowledge abolishes explanation.[2]

In effect, the skill most required and celebrated by this type of quiz is the ability to recall single discrete units of factual knowledge at high speed. It is somewhat ironic that we should, in a cultural form, celebrate the one function of the brain most easily performed, and performed far more efficiently, by computers. This form of quiz then mobilizes not the educated mentality, with its ability to understand and analyse, but the acquisitive instinct that accumulates and stores items of information, just as a squirrel stores nuts. Trivial Pursuits, in its title, acknowledges the ultimate worthlessness of this form of 'knowledge', yet the reverence accorded to people who 'know things' and a relative disinterest in analytic intellect are marked features of the English cultural tradition.

Not all quiz shows draw upon this form of knowledge. The knowledge required in *The Price is Right* is a knowledge of the prices of relatively ordinary domestic luxury goods. Arguably the show validates a social skill not generally given a cultural value, and largely possessed by women rather than men, the skill of bargain hunting acquired by window shopping.[3] Other shows draw on skills other than that of fact retrieval, such as the deduction required in *3–2–1* and *Treasure Hunt*, memory in *The Generation Game*, or the physical and manipulative skills required for parts of *The Krypton Factor*. But what they have in common is that the skill or knowledge can be traded in for prizes. In Tulloch's terms, what you know can be directly translated into 'things'.

However, in the 1980s this traditional form of knowledge was to a degree usurped by a radically different form of knowledge in the highly successful programmes *Play Your Cards Right*, *Family Fortunes*, and *Blankety Blank*. In these game shows, the type of knowledge used as currency is not 'objective fact' but 'public opinion', or knowledge of social discourse. Mills and Rice argue that it is an understanding of the rules of everyday common sense discourse rather than the world of objective and authenticated 'facts' that enables success.[4]

The right answers are not based on absolute fact but by reference to some form of pseudo opinion poll. In *Family Fortunes* a hundred people are asked to name a form of transport, for example, and contestants have to guess those most frequently named. In *Play Your Cards Right*, questions are put to specific groups ('we asked one hundred policemen what they would do if . . .'). In *Blankety Blank* the 'right' answers are determined either by the responses of the panel of celebrities or by the studio audience.

This indicates a marked shift in ideological basis from knowledge as absolute to knowledge as attitude. The knowledge is constructed out of public opinion, albeit of a particular kind, so it is not learning or information, but a grasp of popular common sense that becomes the prerequisite skill. Winners are those who can produce consensual answers, losers produce aberrant answers, so the programmes reward normality and penalize deviance. But they also serve to validate popular 'common sense' as against scientific knowledge. In this sense they dislodge the elitist dominance of 'knowledge' rooted in the class power of those who have been able to acquire a greater quantity of cultural capital. These new populist quizzes dislodge 'expertise' and validate 'what everyone knows'.

In these shows, personality and celebrity come further to the fore. Contestants have to perform themselves, to display their personalities, and indeed on *The Price is Right* are picked for their extrovert qualities. Presenters become celebrities, and other show business celebrities are introduced – as extra production value (*3–2–1*), or as focal point (*Punchlines*, *Celebrity Squares*, *Blankety Blank*).

*Blankety Blank* commences with contestants on one side of the set, and celebrities on the other. Contestants do not walk on; the elaborate machinery of the set wheels them on, and if they lose it wheels them off again. To win through the early stages is to win the right of movement – you get to stand up and be pushed into position by Les Dawson. In achieving final victory, as well as the self-consciously 'cheap' prizes, you win entry into the world of celebrities: the winner is taken over to meet the panel. Television constantly offers, in a variety of programme forms, images of the world of glamour and celebrity. Game shows show ordinary people who with luck can be transported briefly into this world.

Quiz and game shows have featured a broad range of prizes. In *Take Your Pick* and *3–2–1* the prize you win has an element of chance – winning as a lottery. In *Sale of the Century* the prizes are presented in the form of vulgar display – winning as conspicuous consumption. In *The Price is Right* they acquire the appearance of the products of luxury shopping – winning as spending spree. *Blind Date* offers sexuality as a lottery – you win a partner, but one chosen 'blind', while *Mr and Mrs* rewards winners with public confirmation of their compatibility. In *Mastermind, University Challenge*, and *The Krypton Factor* the real prize is status. While the new game shows have prizes, in a sense they are actually not about winning prizes, but are about ordinary people being on television – the real prize is your 15 minutes of fame.[5]

A similar set of differences can be seen to underlie the role of the audience. In the intellectual quizzes the audiences are there primarily as reverent witnesses – the superior skill of the contestants doesn't really admit any active participation. By contrast the more populist quizzes have always actively mobilized audience participation – from the cries of 'take the money/open the box' on *Take Your Pick*, to the shouts of 'higher/lower' on *Play Your Cards Right*, and the general freestyle yelling of *The Price is Right*. And on some of the new game shows the audience is actually the source of knowledge in that it has provided the answers. Clearly television quizzes and game shows also offer a place for an active domestic viewer in that it is possible to compete with the contestants. In this sense the text–viewer relation is significantly different from narrative, though research into audiences has yet to take sufficient account of such differences.

Quizzes have been attacked for being merely a form of celebration of consumption, glorifying consumer goods. On British television, however, it is questionable that the prizes are a central focus. The BBC have never gone in for lavish prizes and indeed the prizes on *Blankety Blank* are a major element in the gentle self-reflexive parody of the whole game show form that is part of *Blankety Blank's* appeal. The IBA limit prize levels on ITV game shows, and the emphasis has generally been more on 'fun and games' than on massive material reward.

Richard Dyer suggests that popular entertainment characteristically offers abundance, energy, and community, in contrast to the scarcity, exhaustion, and isolation more common to lived reality.[6] He argues that entertainment is in this sense often rooted in a utopian sensibility, offering an idealized world from which scarcity, tiredness, and loneliness have been eliminated. While it is in no sense utopian, a show like *The Price is Right* could be seen in these terms, for it is nothing if not exuberant. Everything about the staging of the show is designed to produce the impression of energy and the audience are galvanized into a temporary frenetic community. But it cannot be denied that in the last analysis the experience is structured around the competition to win commodities.

In order to win commodities it is necessary to produce answers and, as already stated, the nature of the answers required has been subject to change. There are distinct ideological shifts at work underlying the role of 'knowledge' in game shows.

The traditional regime of knowledge was being disrupted by the end of the 1970s by the rise of the populist 'we asked one hundred people. . .' form of game show. There are interesting parallels here with broader political and ideological shifts. Many of the traditional assumptions and certainties of post-war Britain were being dismantled by the rise of Thatcherism. In its early populist phase, Thatcherism challenged established political knowledge by reference, mediated through the tabloid press, to the 'common-sense' of ordinary people. During the same period, game shows shifted from a dependence on the traditional empirical/factual model of knowledge, towards a celebration of the views of ordinary people as a source of understanding.

But by the late 1980s, Thatcherism has consolidated its power, and having successfully dismantled the old Butskellite welfare state consensual politics, is in the midst of an active reconstruction of major social institutions. As the project of imposing a new educational orthodoxy gets under way there are signs of a regeneration of the knowledge-as-fact school of quiz.

Can it be entirely without relevance that at least one new game show, *Fifteen to One*, seems rooted in that most competitive of models for education, the Victorian classroom. The presenter (teacher?) William G. Stewart fires a series of questions at his pupils until one by one they are eliminated by failure, leaving one victor. Stewart, in teacherly fashion, presides over this most competitive and hierarchical of educational forms, and it is ironic that he was also responsible for producing *The Price is Right*, in which the cheerfully unruly audience are much more like children let out of school.

It is certainly not the case that a programme like *Fifteen to One* was planned to buttress a return to Victorian values in education. But popular culture is a part of the climate of the times, and indeed does not just reflect it but helps to produce it. So this programme can both be a response to a reassertion of competition in education, but also part of the process by which such attitudes are reproduced. (This is part of the process of hegemony, discussed more fully in chapter 6 by Michael O'Shaughnessy.)


**Sport**

Sports presents us with a different set of problems because, unlike with quizzes, the events portrayed have an existence independent of the cameras.

So while television is relaying the events to us, it is not creating them from scratch. However, as several accounts argue, it does more than simply reflect them to us. By its choice of camera positions and shots, cutting patterns, commentary styles, and by the addition of layers of preliminary discussion and post mortem it is in fact transforming the events, or constructing versions of them.[7] However, the subject can be approached with some of the same questions with which we examined game shows – how is competition represented, what is invested in winning and losing, and what is to be won?

Sport is heavily framed by its television coverage. Extensive airtime is devoted to building up major events – singling out the key stars to watch out for, soliciting the advice of 'experts' as to what will happen, and forging points of identification as a means of winning and holding an audience.

One major appeal of sport is its uncertainty – we do not know what the outcome will be, yet we know there will be a result. So the question 'who will win?' is foregrounded in any sport coverage. Yet if all we needed was to know the result there would be no need to provide more than a result service – clearly there is considerable pleasure in seeing the process of arriving at a result. Sport has a structure not unlike a narrative, and in transforming it into televisual form, the narrative points are further brought out. We follow the story step by step in the progress towards a result. Stars play a major role in putting these stories into focus, and providing points of identification so the Moscow Olympics on British television were dominated by Coe v. Ovett[8] and in the Los Angeles Olympics the Decker v. Budd story provided a major focus.

The notion of winning and losing is integral to sport. Television emphasizes the celebration of winners. Race winners are caught in close up and followed around laps of honour, goal scorers are highlighted and their goals repeated, sometimes *ad nauseam*. Medal ceremonies further serve to underline the cultural importance of victory, and post-mortem interviews aim to catch the victor in the very moment of triumph.

Frequently, losers just disappear from the screen, never to be referred to again. If they are British they will have to go through the ordeal of interview ('I did my best, it just wasn't there. . .') but only rarely, if there has been a major incident (as with Decker or Budd) will the winner be eclipsed for long. The whole language of commentary serves to underline the centrality of winning, of gaining, in Daley Thompson's terms, 'the Big G'.

In international sport, success at sport has long been taken as a symbol of national wellbeing. The sporting failures of the 1950s were taken as a symbol of British world decline, with the famous home football 6–3 defeat by Hungary acquiring the status of a watershed. Similarly the 1966 World Cup victory became a high water mark of national sporting recovery and self-confidence. Patriotic identification with national teams became an easily mobilized force around which to build audience involvement. British competitors and their chances are foregrounded and we are addressed by television as patriotic supporters.

But the peculiar amalgam of nations that the British state constitutes means that many Scottish, Welsh, and Irish viewers merely feel antagonized when invited to identify with the hopes of the English team. England always seems to stand for the whole British nation, whereas the Celtic nations only become 'British' when they are on the verge of success, as Scotland seemed to be before the 1978 World Cup.

Television's need to find some form of national identification for viewers is revealed in the famous remark in a swimming commentary, 'in the absence of a British competitor, our hopes lie with the Australian. . .'. When no British interest is available it is vital to construct for the audience a surrogate-Brit to identify with.

While quiz and game shows are at least partly about material reward, sport coverage is still marked by a contradiction between amateur and professional norms and values. The amateur model of sport stresses competition as an end in itself – it is not a means towards material reward or fame. Some sports – football, cricket, golf, for example – have of course always been professional at their top levels. Others – tennis and athletics – have become professional. But all sports have been subject to a growing professionalization at their top levels. Television has been in part responsible for this – both in directly providing revenue in the form of payments to sport for television rights, and indirectly in triggering off the sponsorship boom. It has also had a significant effect on the nature of sport. One-day cricket and open tennis were in large part prompted by the needs of television. Yet ironically television still seems at times reluctant to acknowledge this professionalization and its consequences. British television-sport commentators, particularly on the BBC, are far more coy about mentioning money and the amount winners get than their counterparts in the USA. More alarmingly they produce remarkably little reportage on the organization of sport, and this during a period when the whole structure of sport is being dramatically transformed.

Success in sport is presented in terms of the acquisition not of money but of fame. Winners rapidly enter into the world of celebrities – appearing in after-match interviews and television advertisements, popping up as experts, appearing on game shows, and generally being 'well known for being well known'. But whereas ordinary people are expected to be content with their 15 minutes of fame, sport stars are often keen to hold onto celebrity status. Of all figures in the public eye, sport stars have the shortest careers and consequently a need to acquire a celebrity status that will outlast their playing careers, as Henry Cooper and Jimmy Greaves have done so decisively.

Such figures are crucial to television's means for winning and holding audiences. Most of the viewers in a large television audience are not sport fans, and it is not by producing an expert-oriented discourse addressing the cognoscenti that their attention can be won. It is vital that television sport successfully delivers entertainment value, and celebrities and personalities are part of the hard currency by which television entertainment values are measured.

This in turn helps to account for the rather contradictory nature of the television evaluation of sport. In devoting a fair amount of time to previews and post mortems of sporting events, television is potentially adopting the role of critic and evaluator. To do so it has to turn to people – players, ex-players, managers, and coaches – who can clearly be offered as providing 'expertise'. But in striving to offer entertainment value, television tends to gravitate towards those experts who are good entertainment value, those who are personalities. So the panel of experts becomes the panel of entertainers and, while the original ITV pundits (Derek Dougan, Pat Crerand, and Brian Clough), became TV stars, the analysis of football seemed to diminish in quality as the stars became more conscious of the imperative to 'perform'. The inheritors of this contradiction are 'Saint and Greavesie' who hover uneasily between an insiders' view of football offered with genuine wit, and a clumsy self-conscious jokiness collapsing into self-parody.

## Quasi-sport

> . . . sporting people tend to gravitate to show business people and vice versa: basically we're all in the same game. (Fred Perry, 1984)

Just as sport and show business have always been closely related, so celebrity and competition have, on television, provided a meeting ground between the two worlds. The term quasi-sport requires a brief explanation.[9] The main aim of this category is to reference that interface between sport as a source of iconography, a model for competitive narrative, and a generator of a star system, and the mainstream of popular peak-time television with its entertainment values, and pressures to win and hold a mass heterogeneous audience. The significance of this meeting of sport and entertainment on the ground of television can be borne out by the range and imagination of the types of programme I include here.

- sports events which include celebrities (*Pro Celebrity Snooker, Pro Celebrity Golf, Around With Alliss*)
- programmes with sport stars not playing their usual sport (*Superstars* and *Superteams*)
- programmes involving celebrities and games (*Star Games*)
- programmes drawing upon sport for iconography and information (*Up for the Cup, A Question of Sport, We Are The Champions, The Record Breakers*)
- programmes involving the general public in games requiring a degree of physical skill (*The Krypton Factor, It's a Knockout, Jeux Sans Frontières, The Golden Shot, Bruce's Big Night, The Generation Game, 3–2–1*).

It is noteworthy that television seems increasingly prepared to turn almost anything into the stuff of competition. Some examples in recent years have been the *World Latin Dance Championships, World Disco Dance Championship, Young Scientist of the Year, Young Musician of the Year, The Great Fishing Race, The Eurovision Song Contest, The Great Egg Race, The*

111

*Great Double Bass Race.* Also relevant here are the broadcasts of award ceremonies such as *Sports Review of the Year*, the Professional Footballers' Award Dinner, and the similar non-sport occasions such as the BAFTA awards and the Academy Awards.

The key factor all these things have in common is the combination of elements of sport and entertainment in a competitive structure. *It's a Knockout* and *Jeux Sans Frontières* were successful in winning large audiences throughout the 1970s with *Jeux Sans Frontières* watched by a staggering 160 million across Europe, and 10 million in Britain. It quite explicitly aimed at non-serious competition:

> Slapstick humour with a hard competitive edge is what the people want. There's too much realism in TV these days. You know the kind of thing: brittle drama series, gloom filled documentaries and sophisticated cynical humour. We're offering people a circus atmosphere and just at the very moment when the atmosphere is tense and full of drama, someone throws a custard pie. (Barney Colehan, *It's a Knockout Annual* 1967)

Here the show is consciously cast in the escapist mould – as the antidote to hard reality – precisely the utopian function of entertainment at work. It is worth noting that *It's a Knockout* rose to the fore amidst a climate of cynical comment to the effect that money and politics were ruining sport. Precisely part of the appeal offered by *It's a Knockout* lay in its difference from real sport: winning was not that important.[10] It offered a magical recovery of the notion of sport as fun and as an end in itself.

*Superstars* was for many years the most successful of the quasi-sports. It started in Britain in 1973, and was shown worldwide by the end of the decade. It began with an emphasis on fun and inadvertent slapstick, but athletes soon began training especially to win it, and a new form of professionalism began to creep in. Ultra-strenuous exercise contests were introduced and the whole event began to demand a particular kind of specialization. In the process some of the point of the event was eroded, as initially it was precisely the lack of ability of an Ian Botham riding a bike or a David Hemery playing football that constituted its appeal.

Of the whole series of pro-celebrity sport events Yorkshire's *Pro Celebrity Snooker* was one of the more successful, in part because of the pleasure of seeing the normal phlegmatic implacability of the professional snooker players threatened by the quips of the celebrities, who were often comics. The players were however quite clear about their responsibility to entertain, indeed concerned to mark that this 'fun' was very different from the serious competitiveness of real snooker:

'Are you going to be able to cope with this?'
*Doug Mountjoy*: 'I think so. . . .It's like light entertainment.'
*Ray Reardon*: 'I think it's going to be a very interesting match, and certainly entertaining.'

But rather than simply a blend between sport and entertainment, the programme actually exploits the contradiction between the rather intense serious concentration and sedate reverent atmosphere of professional snooker, and the irreverent, wisecracking raucousness of the comedians, along with their lack of snooker ability.

Other quasi-sport was far less well judged and often opportunistic. The genre perhaps reached its nadir in 1980 with the *Love Doubles*, a tennis match between John Lloyd and Chris Evert and Bjorn Borg and Marianna Simionescu. The programme used a heart design in the titles and the commentary introduced Bjorn Borg and his fiancée, and Mr and Mrs John Lloyd with the words 'this marvellous event which has excited so much interest in the tennis world and indeed anyone who's interested in romance as well'. It was all part of a gala evening with money going to Princess Anne's charities, but provided neither authentic sport nor pleasurable entertainment. It showed clearly the way that dramatic narrative tension of real competition is an important element in the ability of television sport to hold an audience.

*Britain's Strongest Man* offers an extraordinary appropriation of comic-strip-style images of masculinity. There are extensive echoes of Desperate Dan in the programme: lifting cars, tearing telephone directories in half, bending iron bars on heads. As a counterpoint, Barbara Windsor has in the past been a compère, providing connotations of blonde barmaids with cockney cheek. The programme makes a fetish of physical strength, with sado-masochistic images of the body under stress. The strength and stress required test the body literally to destruction. One man in a car-lifting game collapsed with a damaged back. Strength is reduced to an abstract system of equivalence, measured to two decimal places. Unlike the previous examples, *Britain's Strongest Man* reinstates competition with a vengeance. Yet its representation of gender roles is so self-consciously stereotypical, particularly when set against the changing attitudes to gender set in process by the rise of the women's movement during the 1970s, that it is hard to imagine it being understood by a 1980s audience as anything other than a comic-strip view of life.

In recent years quasi-sport appears to have been in a decline, with the BBC dropping *It's a Knockout* and *Superstars*. It may well be that as real sport is increasingly made to conform to the demands of entertainment the need for forms of quasi-sport has diminished. Similarly, quiz and game shows are not currently quite as popular as they were during the early 1980s, having been dislodged by the rise of soap opera to preeminence in the ratings. But competition in its various forms continues to be a resilient means by which narratives can be produced and audiences won.

## Notes

1 John Fiske and John Hartley, *Reading Television*, London: Methuen, 1978, ch. 10.
2 Tulloch, op. cit. in Further reading.
3 See John Fiske, 'Quizzical pleasures', *Television Culture*, London: Methuen, 1987, ch. 14.
4 Adam Mills and Phil Rice, 'Quizzing the popular', *Screen Education*, no. 41 (Winter/Spring 1982).
5 Jane Root, *Open the Box*, London: Comedia, 1986.
6 Richard Dyer, 'Entertainment and Utopia', *Movie*, no. 24 (1977).
7 Edward Buscombe (ed.), *Football on Television*, London: British Film Institute, 1975.
8 Garry Whannel, 'Narrative and television sport: the Coe and Ovett story', in *Sporting Fictions*, Birmingham: Centre for Contemporary Cultural Studies, University of Birmingham, 1982.
9 As far as I know the term was first devised by Charles Barr in unpublished notes on television sport.
10 Garry Whannel, *'It's a Knockout*: constructing communities' *Block*, no. 6 (1982).

## Further reading

Clarke, Alan, and Clarke, John, 'Highlights and action replays', in Jennifer Hargreaves (ed.), *Sport, Culture and Ideology*, London: Routledge & Kegan Paul, 1982.
Tulloch, John, 'Gradgrind's heirs: the quiz and presentation of "knowledge" by British television', in Geoff Whitty and Michael F. D. Young (eds), *Explorations in the Politics of School Knowledge*, Driffield: Studies in Education, 1977.
Whannel, Garry, 'Fields in vision: sport and representation', *Screen*, vol. 25, no. 3 (1984).

# 8 GENDERED FICTIONS
## Verina Glaessner

Soap opera as a form is more popular than ever. At least five different programmes are regularly listed amongst the top ten audience ratings. The popular press both celebrates and exploits soap operas for their news value – witness the manner in which the personal lives of the stars become mixed almost inextricably with those of the characters they play.

Yet serious critical opinion derides soaps, and their position within the institution of television has traditionally been equally low. Soaps rarely win BAFTA awards. Jean Alexander was nominated for best actress in 1988 after years in the role of *Coronation Street*'s Hilda Ogden, but didn't win. *EastEnders* producer Julia Smith did get an award – but for her whole career in television, rather than for being a soap opera producer.

Daytime soap operas in America and local ones like *Coronation Street* are television's bread and butter, and their budgets, casting, and scheduling reflect this. They are regularly lambasted for the fact that both 'nothing' and 'too much' happens in them.

It is typically assumed that their audience consists of those whose lives are so deprived as to need spurious enrichment. It is portrayed as an aesthetically naive audience, unable to tell fiction from reality. This critical disdain must be related to the structure of the audience which, especially in the case of the daytime and early-evening soap operas, is assumed by programme makers, advertisers, and those producing the attendant publicity material, to be a largely female one. Forms of popular culture consumed mainly by women, such as soap opera, romantic fiction, or bingo have rarely been accorded a high cultural status in the public domain.

Over the past decade or so this low status has been challenged. The soaps have been claimed by some feminists as one of the few areas of television to open up a space for women characters and for an examination of the concerns of women and a representation of the texture of women's lives. The soaps are seen to allow a focus on the area of relationships outside of waged labour, the area that has conventionally been seen as woman's sphere of activity.

Within the genre it is possible to suggest a broad typology. British soap operas, such as ITV's *Coronation Street*, *Crossroads*, the newer *Brookside* (Channel 4) and the BBC's *EastEnders*, are broadly within the tradition of social realism, featuring everyday characters, plots, and language, often located within working-class communities. At the other end of the scale is the romantic and melodramatic world of the United States' exports: *Dallas*, with its offshoots *Knots Landing* and *The Colbys*, and *Dynasty*. In these the 'social' background disappears beneath the expressive excesses of *nouveau riche* wealth, thereby throwing the struggles for power, identity, and family control into relief. Some American commentators make a further distinction between these prime-time programmes and the lower-budget daytime and early-evening soaps, whose titles suggest the world of romantic fiction – *Guiding Light*, *All My Children*, *Search for Tomorrow*.[1] Their preoccupations are, again, with family and identity, rather than the representation of a certain particular social reality.

## History

The daytime soap opera had its origins in American radio with serials during the 1930s often sponsored by major soap manufacturers. Both the serials themselves and the commercials that introduced and punctuated them were directed almost exclusively at a female audience, assumed to be housebound and engaged in domestic chores between 9 a.m. and 3 p.m. These programmes concentrated on female characters, often shown within a professional setting, such as the medical and legal worlds, but with the emphasis on the emotional aspects of the narrative. The same applied in Australia through the late 1940s and 1950s. Many soaps, such as *Dr Paul*, and *Portia Faces Life* (featuring a female lawyer), were broadcast both in the USA and Australia. Other Australian soaps were produced by companies, such as Crawfords, who later went on to produce television series.

116

Britain's first long-running daily serial, *Mrs Dale's Diary*, began transmission in 1948 and ran until 1969. Mrs Dale's position as a doctor's wife proved an uncontroversial way of ensuring a variety of storylines which could cut inoffensively across class boundaries. It was soon followed by the long-running *The Archers*, again with a rural background. In Britain it was not until the 1950s that soap opera transferred to television with *The Groves*, which ran from 1954 to 1957.

*Coronation Street* appeared in 1960 and its consistently high ratings encouraged the development of a number of other soaps and serials, most notably the highly successful hospital series *Emergency Ward Ten*. Other attempts to emulate its success, the BBC's *Compact*, *United*, and *The Newcomers*, were more shortlived. *Crossroads*, developed as a Midlands reply to *Coronation Street*'s northern working-class ambience, was first transmitted in 1964 in the ATV region and soon went national.

Although *Crossroads* had a large and loyal audience the need to make four episodes weekly made for a hectic production schedule and it was never popular with the IBA, who criticized its quality and ordered in 1980 a reduction to three episodes weekly. Rivals appeared – *Brookside* in 1982 and *EastEnders* in 1986 – and in 1987 it was decided to end *Crossroads* permanently. Its genesis and development are recounted by Dorothy Hobson.[2]

The American soap opera *Dallas*, first screened as a limited series in April 1976, rapidly gained international distribution. Its parent company also produces *Falcon Crest* and *Knots Landing*. Like ABC's *Dynasty*, it is scheduled for peak viewing in America in the 9 p.m. weekday slot opposite sit-coms like *Family Ties*, or NBC's *Hill Street Blues*.

Despite its generally low status as a genre, soap opera is a valuable form for winning reliably high ratings. Almost by definition the genre commands strong audience loyalty. It is not necessary to watch every episode, but there is a strong incentive to watch regularly enough to stay in touch with the narrative. Quiz and game shows may well have high ratings but only occasionally does their format itself encourage this kind of 'product loyalty'. The pleasures offered by the soap operas stem from the points of identification offered by their characters. We want to discover what happens to those specific characters locked into that specific network of relationships. This audience loyalty is sometimes sustained over a period of a decade or more.

Low status necessitates small budgets (except for peak-time soap operas). The same sets are used repeatedly, and in the cases of the Australian soaps *The Young Doctors*, or *Neighbours*, or the British serial *Crossroads*, the sets have often been rudimentary. Directing and producing have been looked on as apprentice work and often paid accordingly. There are however, signs that the success of *Dallas* and its spawn and the current massive popularity of the genre has begun to change the commercial status of the genre.

## What is a soap opera?

First of all a distinction can be made between series and serials. While series feature the same characters regularly, each individual programme has its own discrete storyline, generally resolved by the end of the programme. Serials, by contrast, may have stories resolved within one episode but have at least one storyline that continues from episode to episode. In limited-episode serials, which may run for six, twelve, or more episodes, this narrative is resolved by the final episode. Soap opera, by contrast, is an indefinite serial that in theory can continue for ever. Commonly soap operas feature multiple and interlocking narratives, some of which may be shortlived, while others go on for months or even years. Ultimate narrative closure is indefinitely postponed – in this sense soap opera is open-ended as opposed to the characteristic closed narrative form of situation comedy.

In the soap opera, as one set of problems is resolved another begins its gestation. In *EastEnders* from May to August 1986 the paternity of Michelle's baby became an issue, there was the case of the poisoning of the dog Rowley, and the beginning of an affair. At the end of an episode certain problems may near resolution, while others develop. We may typically be left with a cliffhanger, a moment of revelation or suspense, or merely a thought-provoking image, but in all cases narrative questions are left open, and closure is postponed.

The kind of answer we give to the 'what next' provoked by the soap opera hinges less on a simple schedule of events and more on questions formed around the effects certain actions will have on the characters. In a series like *Minder* the end of an episode leaves us with the narrative wound up and the relationship between the protagonists re-established. We can look forward to a new adventure with the same protagonists. In a situation comedy, like *George and Mildred* or *Man About the House*, the end of one episode and the beginning of the next find the central characters largely unchanged. They have not accumulated a history, nor do they generally acquire a memory of what has happened in previous episodes.

By contrast, while soap characters may not change substantially, they do acquire an accretion of experience, shared and understood by the regular viewer, as well as recollections of events, which we may not have witnessed, but which are recalled for us. So just as soap characters have a continuing existence, with an uncertain future around which our identification with the narrative is forged, so they also have a past, a history, in which to a degree we have participated. This awareness of the history in a programme is a major source of pleasure, enabling viewers both to share and exchange information about the past and, on the basis of this knowledge, to anticipate the future: to 'read ahead' of the narrative.

## Pleasure and gender

The pleasures of soap opera hinge on the particular relationship established between narrative and character. According to the expectations brought to an action series or an adventure serial, 'nothing' seems to happen in a soap like *Coronation Street* or *Brookside* because the satisfactions gained reside elsewhere than in a fast-flowing sequence of narrative events. The repercussions events will have on the lives of the characters are brought to the fore. This. is registered largely through talk – through gossip, confessions, speculations, and exchanges of confidence.

Conventionally the world of gossip is seen as a woman's world, existing as part of the realm of the domestic and personal. Within this context the world of work becomes another arena for exhibiting a concern for people and their problems – it is humanized. Typically work within realist soaps is within the service industries – pubs, shops, and launderettes (although see below with reference to *Coronation Street*), which produce naturalized settings for the exchange of gossip.

Soaps also tend to focus on female characters not as the mysterious or peripheral figures of crime and action series but as everyday people coping with the problems of life. Christine Geraghty argues that they constitute the norm against which we test the behaviour of characters, and through whom we experience events.[3]

While audiences consist of both men and women, some writers have argued that the soap opera genre speaks specifically to women – the gender of the viewer is inscribed in the text.[4] This is because they draw upon and speak to the specific skills attendant upon finding the mainspring of one's existence within the world of the personal and private and within the knowledge of the conventions of personal life that this brings. Charlotte Brunsdon argues that it is in gossip, the repeated mulling over of actions and possibilities, that the moral and ideological frameworks adhere. Modes of behaviour are tested and explored through talk: will she marry or not? Will she tell or not? It is not a crime that is being investigated but possible modes of behaviour. Dorothy Hobson suggests that women characteristically use such programmes to talk, indirectly, about their own lives and their own attitudes.

While critics argue that nothing happens in the British social realist soaps, they frequently level the very opposite criticism at the more melodramatic American soaps, in which 'too much happens'. In such programmes there is indeed typically an over-plenitude, derived from the location of a multiplicity of narratives around a permanent family of characters.

In *Dallas*, which some prefer to label a melodramatic serial,[5] J.R.'s business deals are important, not in the way they might be within a dynastic chronicle or an exposé of capitalism, but as indices of his character – examples of his power and deviousness and expressions of his relationship with other characters. As the core of the genre is the private world, attendant rituals of family life, births, marriages, divorces, and romances come to the fore, and because of the nature of the genre these rituals become a source of uncertainty, worry, confusion, doubt, and threat rather than resolution, reassurance, or closure. If a classically socially-oriented British soap opera like *Coronation Street* can be seen to be about the 'settling of people in life' a prime-time American soap like *Dallas* could be understood as being precisely about the unsettling of its characters, its realism coming not through documentation of ordinary life, but through scrutinizing the emotional urgency that underpins all family life.

The pleasures available from any generic text depend in part upon one's familiarity with its conventions – to what extent are they adhered to, stretched, or contravened? The pleasures available from the soap opera also by definition depend upon a certain amount of knowledge of that specific programme. To catch the full implications of certain scenes in *EastEnders* we have to know who the father of Michelle's baby is. We must also have an interest as well as a competence in handling the conventions of personal life, and competence within this area belongs, it is argued, especially to women.

## Soap: audience and realism

*Coronation Street* commenced broadcasting in 1960 and has been in continual production ever since. It is a key soap opera in the context of British television not only because of its popularity but also for the way it poses questions relating to the representation of the working class, and particularly of working-class women, within popular culture.

As Richard Dyer points out in his introduction to the BFI monograph,[6] *Coronation Street* is the product of the same historical moment as Richard Hoggart's *The Uses of Literacy*.[7] This book, together with other sociological works, novels, films, and plays of the late 1950s, was concerned to reveal and legitimize working-class culture. Hoggart both celebrated this culture and took a stand against the corruption of its traditional values.

Hoggart's book, based as it was on his own upbringing in the 1930s, was characterized by a degree of nostalgia. Similarly *Coronation Street*, while celebrating and validating aspects of working-class culture and everyday life, tended to locate its image of this world in somewhat nostalgic terms. As the programme's image of community remained rather rooted in the period of the programme's conception, it has appeared increasingly nostalgic for an (imaginary) past, and has had trouble incorporating and representing the processes of change of work within inner-city communities during the 1970s and 1980s.

This magical recovery of an organic (and almost entirely white) working-class community is, it must be assumed, a significant element in its appeal. The image is of course partial – Hoggart's account was one in which, as Dyer points out, work itself, labour, and industrial relations were largely omitted, and in the programme class has always appeared more as a matter of 'lifestyle' than as a set of social relations. As in Hoggart's account the emphasis on home and the domestic gives a prominence to the everyday, to common sense, and to the lives of women. The programme played a major role in establishing the conventions by which social realism was articulated in the form of soap opera.

Social realism demands the suggestion of unmediated access to the real world, the real world being understood as the terrain of the ordinary and the everyday. Marion Jordan examines the close fit achieved between social realism, with its emphasis on social problems explored through the personal, and the conventions of the soap opera:

> though. . .events are ostensibly about social problems, they should have as one of their central concerns the settling of people in life. . .the resolution of these events should always be in terms of the effects of personal interventions.[8]

*Coronation Street* can be seen to be definitively about the 'settling of people in life' as well as being a celebration of commonsensical working-class culture. This culture provides the fabric of the programme: the communal gathering in pub and café, and the popping in and out of people's houses. Industrial labour is largely absent, or present only vestigially in memory and history.

The one site of industrial labour prominently featured is Mike Baldwin's clothing factory. Based almost entirely on a labour force of women, it has provided a setting for boss–worker relations, including a running story around a strike and resolution, which is discussed in the BFI monograph. But class, in adherence to an older literary tradition, has been rendered in terms of 'pithy' characters like Ena Sharples, Albert Tatlock, Hilda Ogden, and Bet Lynch, rather than in terms of class relations or antagonisms.

One of the most striking characteristics of *Coronation Street* is its privileging of the social and communal over the familial. The archetypal nuclear family is absent and its absence forces attention onto the area of social interaction and exchange. The characters function within the community, however limited this community might be, rather than the home, within a semi-public sphere rather than within the fraught hothouse of family relationships. *EastEnders* shows a similar bias but at the same time makes a clear space for the discussion of family life, in particular around the traditional extended Fowler family of which Michelle is a part. Other characters are also placed within families as well as being part of the life of the square.

The borders of the community in *Coronation Street* are staunchly patrolled and those who attempt to move beyond its circumscribed boundaries are not encouraged. Deirdre Langton is assaulted when she attempts to move beyond its limitations, Len Fairclough dies on his way back from a secret affair, and only Ken and Mike have voiced aspirations that would take them beyond its boundaries (and neither have been successful).

The shelving of the family opens up the terrain of the social for exploration but it was only during the producership of Susi Hush (1974–6) that there was a move in the direction of the wider social and political world, signalled by the first brief introduction of a black character and the news of Bet Lunch's hitherto unknown son's death in Northern Ireland. While the introduction of tougher, more contemporary social themes was an interesting move, audience figures dropped, and after Bill Podmore's appointment as producer, this shift has been reversed, with a decisive move towards a lighter, more humorous tone. As current producer John Temple put it, 'we are in the business of entertaining, not offending' (*Broadcast*, 20 December 1985).

There are signs of attempts to update *Coronation Street*, partly in response to the arrival on the scene of *EastEnders* and *Brookside*, by introducing more young characters, although all have now been outstripped by *Neighbours* which has found great success by addressing the young audience.

It has been argued, however, that the refusal to foreground the thematic of the family has given *Coronation Street* an unmatched opportunity to represent independent female characters existing as individuals within a community rather than as members of a family, as happens for instance in *Brookside*. They are also granted, Terry Lovell argues, a sexuality that is allowed to continue into middle age rather than becoming subsumed within family concerns.[9]

The tension between public acclaim and critical hostility was thrown into sharp relief by the demise of *Crossroads*. Dorothy Hobson draws attention to the contrast between the exceptionally high ratings of the programme and the critical attitude of both journalists and the IBA. She argues that broadcasters should not despise popular programmes or their audiences, and asserts that a soap opera which appeals to and connects with the experiences of 15 million people is 'as valid and as valuable as a work of art or as a single play or documentary which may attract four million viewers' (p. 171).

This point of view constitutes a welcome attack on cultural elitism, but by this analysis gladiatorial combat, if popular, would also be endorsed. Hobson fails to distinguish between a programme's sociological interest and its aesthetic merits, deriving her aesthetic judgements primarily from the place and function of the programme within the lives of its viewers. This does, however, raise questions as to the importance of the pleasures of viewing. She sees *Crossroads* as uniting character and viewer on the common ground of everyday experience and common sense, and as speaking to, and about, working-class and *petit-bourgeois* women within the terms of social realism and the ideology of common sense. The values posed are personal and domestic, far removed from heroism or adventure, and it is within the privileging of this realm in the particular ways open to the soap opera that the pleasures afforded by *Crossroads* were rooted.

But common sense is precisely ideological – a partial understanding of the world. *Brookside* producer, Phil Redmond, signalled a more analytic intention when he declared that *Brookside* would 'tell the truth and show society as it really is', recalling realism to its social base in 'issues' and 'problems'.

Like *Coronation Street*, *Brookside* has a northern location, in a newly built housing estate on the fringes of Liverpool. The serial's much discussed authenticity is there to underscore the veracity of its characters and the pointedness of its social critique, the topicality of which Redmond sees as the peculiar province of the soap. Redundancy, union organization, the legal system, gambling, prostitution by housewives, infertility, the Church, have all fallen within the broad net of the serial's scripts.

But realism has also provided something of a stick with which to beat it. *Brookside* has been criticized for placing its characters in a situation of relative affluence when in reality Liverpool has some of the worst housing conditions in Europe. It 'replaces *Coronation Street*'s outmoded working class characters with baseless stereotypes who exist in a political vacuum' according to Kevin Sutcliffe (*City Limits*, 30 November 1984).

Realism has always been seen as a trap for its female characters. Christine Geraghty[10] argues that the setting, the separate houses of the close, function to push the female characters out of the community and into the home. The women have then to be brought into contact with each other through the deliberate action of the narrative. She cites the independence of Emily Bishop and Elsie Tanner in *Coronation Street* and opposes them to Sheila Grant, especially in the early episodes of *Brookside* where she operates principally as the comforter of her husband.

Geraghty also argues that the weight of dramatic interest in this serial is deflected from its female characters in a way that renders it akin to 'drama proper', which elbows aside the particular pleasures to be gained from the intricate plotting and charting of action and reaction that allows space for domestic concerns.

*EastEnders* was also launched on the claim of greater realism. Julia Smith, the producer, in an interview in *Television Weekly* (30 November 1984) emphasized that *EastEnders* was to be about 'today', about 'everyday life', and that it was to be as topical and documentary as possible. It had to be, she argued, as real in today's terms as *Coronation Street* was when it started.

The initial episodes were bleakly shocking, offering a fairly relentlessly dark, lower-depths study of a post-industrial Britain of unremitting sourness. It struck chords familiar from the best days of the BBC's *Play for Today* and certainly in its gritty realism went beyond anything previously attempted for mass-market viewing.

The similarities with *Coronation Street* are there but to an extent the tables have been turned. Young characters are given far greater prominence and are drawn with some vigour. They are also frequently given the role of recalling their elders to the path of conventional morality (a role familiar from melodrama). *EastEnders* has learnt from American soaps the value of family dramas, and questions of paternity, adoption, fidelity, and so on are played to the hilt. Through its attempts to mobilize the 'real' and the 'topical' alongside the drama of the family, it has a sharper edge, while still staying within the constraints of social realism.[11]

## Soap as melodrama

The byzantine relationships that are played out among the super-elite of *Dallas, The Colbys*, or *Dynasty* would seem to have little in common with the familiar drabness of the everyday world of British soaps. You have to look hard to find traces of the geographical Dallas within the serial. These soaps, too, are about family relationships and it is no accident that two of the three choose titles that directly reference the family, used as the basis for epic melodrama.

*Dallas* focuses on the oil-rich Ewing family and their rivalry with the Barnes family. There are a number of interpenetrations of the two families which, as Dave Kehr points out in *Film Comment* (15, no. 4 (July–August 1979), 66–8), poses a constant threat to their integrity. These conflicts are played out against a whole series of oppositions of country/city, industrial/rural, domestic/commercial, with, in the background and in the titles, a sense of the vanished West and its codes. This already fissured environment serves as a means of magnifying the drama of family life.

Ien Ang argues that

> Women in soap operas never rise above their problematic positions. On the contrary they completely identify with them. In spite of all their miseries they continue to believe in the ideals of patriarchal ideology. . .the patriarchal status quo is non-viable but remains intact.[12]

What melodrama and the melodramatic soaps explore is the struggle that takes place within them. It is a struggle to which the family is central. This is why it is no more relevant to complain that *Dallas* is only about the wealthy than it would be to grumble that *King Lear* is only about royalty.

Jane Feuer traces the origin of prime-time soaps to film melodramas like Douglas Sirk's *Written on the Wind*, which also uses what she calls a process of intensification by which the subject of the film becomes not the events themselves but the emotions these events arouse.[13] These emotions are expressed through opulent sets and costumes and a rhetorical

125

shooting style which forces the characters constantly away from 'ordinariness' and the 'everyday' and towards an emblematic goodness or evil. *Dynasty* interestingly focuses on a female villain but lacks the intensity of writing and sense of multi-layered meanings that characterize *Dallas*. One notable feature of *EastEnders*, at least while Dirty Den and Angie provided the central focus, was the attempt to emulate the emotional flamboyance of *Dallas* while remaining true to its social realist roots.

The emotions that, in this analysis, become the subject of the serial are grounded within the family. Identity becomes something fought for, and over, in relation to the constraints of family life, and motherhood, marriage, and sexuality become dangerous counters in the game rather than issues within a social setting.

Discussion of the soap opera as a genre has come primarily from two different areas: that of film study which has tended towards a theoretical study of the text itself and the possibilities the genre might offer for a progressive reading, and that of television studies which has placed more emphasis on the institutional context. This latter frequently involves taking the empirical existence of a female audience as a starting point. A more theoretically oriented study could involve locating a position inscribed within the text itself, which would apply regardless of the gender of the particular viewer.

The soap opera could be seen as embodying a distinctively 'feminine' way of seeing or being. A key statement in the debate around gender and pleasure in relation to visual texts is Laura Mulvey's 'Visual pleasure and narrative cinema'.[14] This looks at the way in which a narrative positions the viewer, regardless of sexual identity, within a system of visual pleasure set up according to a particular masculine point of view. Mulvey is discussing mainstream Hollywood narrative cinema, but, in extending this direction of analysis, Tania Modleski argues that soaps are not only 'made for' women but that, through the closeness with which they reproduce the world of the private and the domestic, they construct a position for the viewer that accords with feminine rather than patriarchal desire.[15]

For the implications of a genre like soap opera, made for and watched by women, to be explored, it is necessary to look at the ways in which the conventions of social realism and melodrama are articulated. In Britain the form is currently more popular than ever and a full understanding of the ways in which it structures popular consciousness can reveal much about the relation between televisual representation and broader social processes.

# Notes

1 For a discussion of American daytime soaps, see Carol Lopate, 'Daytime television: you'll never want to leave home', *Radical America* (January–February 1977), and Tania Modleski, 'The search for tomorrow in today's soap operas', *Film Quarterly*, vol. 33, no. 1 (1979).
2 Dorothy Hobson, op. cit. in Further reading.
3 Christine Geraghty, in R. Dyer *et al.*, op. cit. in Further reading.
4 Charlotte Brunsdon, '*Crossroads*: notes on a soap opera', *Screen*, vol. 22, no. 4 (1981); Tania Modleski, *Loving With a Vengeance*, op. cit. in Further reading; Modleski, op. cit.
5 Ien Ang's discussion of *Dallas*, in her book *Watching Dallas*, op. cit. in Further reading, discusses these terms fully.
6 The piece by Richard Dyer in Dyer *et al.*, op. cit.
7 Richard Hoggart, *The Uses of Literacy*, London: Penguin, 1958.
8 Marion Jordan's chapter in Dyer *et al.*, op. cit.
9 Terry Lovell's chapter in Dyer *et al.*, op. cit.
10 Christine Geraghty, 'Brookside – no common ground', *Screen*, vol. 24, nos 4–5 (July–October 1983).
11 See David Buckingham, *Public Secrets: EastEnders and its Audience*, London: British Film Institute, 1987.
12 Ang, op. cit.
13 Jane Feuer, 'Melodrama, serial form and television', *Screen*, vol. 25, no. 1 (January–February 1984).
14 Laura Mulvey, 'Visual pleasure and narrative cinema', *Screen*, vol. 16, no. 3 (Autumn 1975).
15 Modleski, *Loving With a Vengeance*.

# Further reading

Ang, Ien, *Watching Dallas*, London: Methuen, 1986.
Dyer, Richard, *et al., Coronation Street*, London: BFI TV Monograph, 1981.
Hobson, Dorothy, *Crossroads: The Drama of a Soap Opera*, London: Methuen, 1982.
Modleski, Tania, *Loving With a Vengeance: Mass Produced Fantasies for Women*, London: Shoe String Press, 1982.

# 9 ONLY WHEN I LAUGH
## Mick Bowes

In an episode from the second series of the BBC situation comedy *The Young Ones* we find references being made to the very nature of sit-com itself:

> *Vyvyan* (referring to *The Good Life*): 'It's so bloody nice. . . . Felicity treacle Kendal and Richard sugar-flavoured snot Briars. . . . They're nothing but a couple of reactionary stereotypes confirming a myth that everyone in Britain is a loveable middle-class eccentric and I hate them.'[1]

It is of course unlikely that many viewers of sit-com would react in quite the same way as Vyvyan. What it does highlight, however, is the way in which a critical awareness of television programmes such as sit-coms is actually creeping into some of the programmes themselves! *The Young Ones* is of course not typical of situation comedy on television and the programme it refers to, *The Good Life*, is a more typical example of the situation comedy format.

Unlike the anarchic parody of *The Young Ones*, which frequently breaks and plays with the conventions of the form, most situation comedy is realist in characters, settings, stories, and language. By looking at the ways in which sit-com presents us with 'real' people in 'real' situations we can begin to see how they fit into our picture of the society we live in.

Television situation comedies usually last for half an hour, are on at the same time, on the same evening each week, and each series lasts for a fixed number of episodes (usually between six and thirteen). Programmes contain the same main characters and usually the same locations each week, and each episode is a self-contained narrative which is resolved at the end of the programme.

Because the episodes are meant to link together and are shown in a particular sequence they can refer to events or characters in previous episodes. This is very different from other forms of comedy on television which are usually made up of a series of unrelated sketches or 'turns' by comedians.

Sit-coms have always used established comic performers already well known to audiences but they now also often use 'straight' actors and actresses in the roles of the main characters. The ways in which characters represent, often in stereotypical fashion, recognizable social types, provide a base for both the humour and the underlying ideology of the form.

The most characteristic feature of the 'classic' situation comedy is narrative closure. In other words, each story is resolved within the 30 minutes of the programme. In addition this closure is generally circular – it returns the characters to the positions they occupied at the start, thus allowing the next week's programme to start afresh. This circular narrative closure allows little room for progression, making situation comedy radically distinct from soap opera as a form, and prompting some to label it a conservative form.

It is certainly true that many sit-coms appear to be about entrapment – characters unable to escape the constraints of their class, their social position, their gender, their marital status, or simply themselves. Hancock can never transcend railway cuttings, Harold Steptoe can never escape from his father, Mildred's upwardly mobile desires are forever frustrated by George's dogged and defensive working-class manner, the housewife in *Butterflies* can never quite bring herself to have an affair with her prospective lover, the father in *Home to Roost* will never quite be able to throw his teenage son out.

At the same time the history of situation comedy clearly shows that the genre is constantly having to handle areas of social unease. Many of the best sit-coms of the 1960s – *Hancock, Steptoe and Son, The Likely Lads* – were in part about class and social mobility or the lack of it. In the wake of the rise of the women's movement in the 1970s, heightened debate about gender roles, and the supposed threat to traditional family structures, came the appearance of new sit-coms focusing on gender relations and the nature of the family – such as *Butterflies, Solo, Agony*. More recent foregrounding of the politics of race in the wake of heightened inner-city tensions is also echoed in programmes such as *Empire Road* and *No Problem*. This is not to say that any of these are either progressive or reactionary, but rather to suggest that, just as humour is often a way of handling unease, so sit-com is often a way in which social unease is re-presented – often in a less threatening manner.

Situation comedy in Britain evolved from radio comedy which in turn had its roots in music hall and variety. American sit-com developed from radio 'soap operas', weekly drama series which were devised to attract audiences in order to sell products. The domestic setting predominated in both variations of the form. Many early American sit-coms were transferred from radio to television, but the most successful one was *I Love Lucy*, created in the 1950s especially for television.

The first major success for British television sit-com came in the late 1950s when *Hancock's Half Hour* was transferred from radio. When Hancock parted with his writers, Galton and Simpson, in the early 1960s the BBC offered them the chance to write six one-off situation comedies in a series, *Comedy Playhouse*. Out of this came another great success, *Steptoe and Son*, the first sit-com to use straight actors (Harry H. Corbett and Wilfred Brambell) rather than comic performers. This was to be the first of a series of successes, such as *The Likely Lads* and *Till Death Us Do Part* that enabled the BBC to dominate the early development of the form in Britain. Apart from a few early successes, such as *The Army Game*, it was not until the end of the 1960s that ITV began to compete more successfully.[2]

While the most common situation has continued to be a domestic one, many of the popular hits of the 1970s and 1980s, such as *Are You Being Served?*, *Dad's Army*, *Hi-De-Hi*, and *'Allo 'Allo*, were based around a work setting, allowing a greater range of regular character types. Struggling against the formal limitations of the genre, many writers began pushing towards the serial, introducing narrative lines that continued from one episode to the next, sometimes across a whole series. *The Rise and Fall of Reginald Perrin*, *Butterflies*, *Agony*, and the American soap opera parody, *Soap*, all had a degree of seriality in their form, and in this sense the question as to whether they really are situation comedies in the traditional sense has to be considered.

Similarly, programmes in other genres sometimes introduce forms of comic exchange and characterization that clearly owe much to sit-com. The interplay between Terry and Arthur in *Minder*, Rita and Mavis in *Coronation Street*, and even Saint and Greavesie, because they play on our familiarity with regular characters and their habits, would appear to have elements derived from the sit-com.

Situation comedy is classified by the television companies as a form of light entertainment, and as such it is something that they think need not be taken too seriously. This has led some writers of situation comedy to feel that their programmes are not given the status they deserve considering how popular they are. This is partially to do with the history of sit-com and its development as a peculiar hybrid of popular drama and variety. Its classification by the television companies as light entertainment rather than drama is indicative of its status. Comic drama has a long tradition and carries with it the status of 'great literature', whereas situation comedy is very much a new form of entertainment and is therefore more difficult to categorize. The main function of TV sit-com according to the television companies is to make people laugh or offer a temporary escape from the worry of everyday life.[3]

In contrast, a report produced by the Department of Education and Science in 1983, *Popular Television and Schoolchildren*, concludes:

> It is important, particularly for teachers, to avoid falling into the trap of conferring greater value per se on programmes which set out to educate and inform them on those whose primary aim is to entertain. . . . For a minority of children the products of television may be the main source of significant influence on the way in which their images of certain groups develop.[4]

In other words, entertainment such as sit-com cannot be discussed as mere escapism, as though its actual content were of no relevance.

Although the television companies themselves do not seem to take sit-com that seriously, it is valuable to them as a means of attracting large audiences. Because of their popularity, the television companies often show them in the early part of the evening in the hope that they will attract large numbers of viewers who will continue to watch the channel for the rest of the evening.

This positioning of programmes in the television company's schedule is important as the number of viewers is reflected in the weekly audience ratings, and the popularity of programmes is important in relation to funding (either from advertisers or justifying increases in the licence fee).

Early evening tends to be a time when 'families' watch programmes together. This notion of the family as a socially cohesive unit is something that is used within the framework of many situation comedy programmes, whether showing the model couple, such as *Terry and June*, or more usually a family situation which is undergoing some form of disruption, such as *Agony* or *No Problem*.

Very few sit-coms present us with the 'perfect' family, but there is often a clear underlying assumption that the perfect family model is a desirable one to aspire towards. Sit-coms usually present us with a 'problematic' family situation which is either resolved through the comedy or is used as a source of humour, with 'normality' seen as the ultimate goal.

As sit-com is so popular it tends to be caught in a trap of repeating previously pleasurable experiences rather than breaking out into something completely different:

> Because of the difficulties of sustaining a comedy series, most of the pressure for satisfying TVs insatiable appetite falls on a small group of experienced writers. Established formats, often based on familiar situations and using well known actors with which the viewers can identify, are among the most popular comedies.[5]

This safe approach to sit-com on the part of the television companies means that it is difficult to present a radically different sit-com. Occasionally, however, new writers are given a chance and programmes such as *The Young Ones* appear which break new ground.

## Realism and location

Mick Eaton outlines three possible locations in which situation comedy can take place. The first is the home and is generally based around a family situation. The second is the workplace and the situations that occur as a result of interaction between characters in the work situation. The third area is less clearly definable, but 'betrays structural elements of both the home and the work paradigms and usually concerns a group of diverse people somehow connected in a situation outside that of their workplace. It usually concerns the home but not the family except tangentially.'[6] Eaton cites as examples *Man About the House*, *Rising Damp*, and *Come Back Mrs Noah*.

The family and work have traditionally been seen as 'normal' in our society. Marriage, children, and living together as a 'nuclear' family are accepted social norms, which although challenged by many people are still the kinds of situations that the majority of people aspire towards.

Sit-com sometimes presents us with a variety of 'families' which are deficient in some way and this lack of wholeness is used as a source of humour. In *No Problem* for example the children are left to run the home after the parents return to the West Indies; *Me and My Girl* is about a single-parent father bringing up his daughter, and *Relative Strangers* is about a father who has just discovered he has a teenage son. Although they present alternatives to the 'normal' family, they do not really challenge it as an institution. Television has simply drawn upon the tensions inherent in the 'abnormality' of these situations as a source for comedy. The increasing appearance of sit-coms that deal with 'non-typical' family groups can, however, be seen as suggesting that social tensions around the concept of the nuclear family are being addressed, and handled in various ways, by sit-coms, from the upholding of a 'single' way of life in *Solo*, to the matriarchal attempts to hold a family together in *Bread*.

Other sit-coms, such as *Agony*, present a whole range of 'problems' within one series. We might find humour in the situations because we identify with the liberal attitudes expressed in the programme, but we might also be opposed to them and find the characters laughable. Much sit-com works across the boundary between normality and deviance. *Agony* does so in a complex manner, by attempting to position the audience so that deviance becomes acceptable, and normality comic. The extent to which it succeeds in this has been the subject of some discussion.[7]

Work is also still considered as something that it is desirable to have, both socially and as a source of income. However, increasing levels of unemployment and changes in the kinds of jobs that need to be done are leading to shifts in attitudes towards work. Sit-coms which use the workplace as their location introduce all kinds of opportunities for exploring relationships between characters. The hierarchical structure of the work environment allow challenges to power, authority, and class position between workers and management and occasionally the customers (such as in *Are You Being Served?*).

Although many of these sit-coms are about the reversal of power relationships and the notion of the underdog triumphing over authority, the locations are usually confined to small and often badly run organizations. Questions of power reversals in larger organizations such as multinational companies are rarely addressed.

Of the sit-coms that centre around some form of workplace (*Are You Being Served?*, *Dad's Army*, *Hi-De-Hi*. *It Ain't Half Hot Mum*, *'Allo 'Allo*, for instance) two points should be made. First many of them are the work of the writers David Croft and Jimmy Perry, and, second, they are almost all set in the past. The workplace location provides for a wider range of interactions between characters while the use of the past addresses the audience through nostalgia and for the older members of the audience it also mobilizes popular memory.

It could be argued that, viewed nostalgically, the world seems safe, funny, or even innocent. But, as always, we read the past through the assumptions of the present. The question then is whether we laugh at the way in which, for example, the workforce in *Brass* are exploited by the evil capitalist Bradley Hardacre only because we think social conditions have changed, or because we recognize a parody of worker–management relations of continuing relevance.

There are several sit-coms which are set in the home but are not centred around a family. These usually involve people who through their circumstances are forced to share their living environment, such as the prisoners in *Porridge* or the students in *The Young Ones*. Here the comedy is often derived from the problems associated with communal living, and even when there is no traditional family structure certain characters may take on specific roles. In *The Young Ones*, for example, much of the humour revolves around domestic issues such as cooking and cleaning. Neil, the hippy, takes on the role of 'mother' in the house by taking responsibility for cooking and shopping, and in return he is not only taken for granted, but is often the focal point of abuse from the others.

How realistic a sit-com can be depends very much on how we perceive the realism of the life it is attempting to portray. If the characters and locations are recognizable then it is easier to accept the situations as they develop. By using 'real' domestic or work situations, sit-coms can often lure us into an acceptance of some of the things contained within the narrative and the humour. If sit-coms stray from these accepted rules and conventions they begin to disturb their audiences. *The Young Ones* was an interesting example of a sit-com that deliberately set out to question a realistic form of narrative. It used the characters and locations from sit-com, but disrupted the narrative flow through absurd or unusual divisions such as talking rats or bands playing in the living room. It could of course be argued that this is not really sit-com as it does not adhere strictly to the conventions of the genre.

## Characters, stereotypes, and politics

Because television situation comedies are fairly short, the identities of characters need to be established as quickly as possible. Although writers may argue that their characters are based on real people, it is often necessary for them to use stereotypes – that is, characters who conform to patterns of behaviour that are easily recognized and understood.

The danger of using stereotypes is that they often present a one-sided viewpoint (generally that of the dominant culture), which fails to challenge the way in which we perceive groups and individuals.[8] We carry around in our heads images of types of people which have been formed by what we have seen and experienced. Some of these images may have been formed through direct first-hand experience, others may have been drawn from secondary sources such as television.

Sit-com draws upon these images in order to present us with easily recognizable characters and also uses these character traits as a source of humour. It is therefore possible to find humour in groups as diverse as mothers-in-law, feminists, gays, and bank managers. The main difference is that although all of these groups may be seen in a negative way in sit-com, in real life some of them have more power than others. Stereotyping is therefore not quite as simple as it first appears. Some groups will always be presented in a negative way, others who portray more socially acceptable forms of behaviour will be seen in a more positive light. People do not necessarily have to conform to stereotypes, but it clearly helps an audience to relate to them quickly if they do. Some of the main characters may have individual characteristics, but other characters fall into more easily recognizable character types.

In a form which attempts to establish character and narrative and produce humour all in a half-hour it is inevitable that characterization will tend towards the stereotypical. In many senses stereotypes are both simple and complex – they are simplified ways of conveying distinct cultural images. In many senses what is important is to examine the place of the stereotype in the structure of the programme – is the stereotype the target of humour or the producer of it? Are we laughing at the stereotyped group or with it? In this sense there is a considerable difference between the crude racist stereotypes of Asian characters in *It Ain't Half Hot Mum*, who we are invited to laugh at, and the gay stereotypes of *Agony* who often function as a means of making the prejudices of 'straight' people seem odd and laughable.

Clearly, images of men and women in television situation comedies are meant to present viewers with types of characters that they can easily recognize and relate to. What they also do however is to retain traditional images of men and women in gender-related roles. Sit-com rarely challenges any of these traditions through the characters and situations it uses. Even more 'progressive' sit-coms such as *Girls on Top*, where all of the main characters are women, fail to present a challenge to traditional role models. The one character who presents a feminist viewpoint is inevitably seen as a 'loony' who no one wants to take seriously.

Part of the problem may be that most writers of sit-com are men, and even when they aim to avoid sexism in their humour they still find it easier to write for male characters.[9] Women rarely get strong roles in sit-coms compared to soaps where there are many powerful women characters.

It could be argued that sit-com is not the right vehicle for challenging such representations and stereotyping. It could, however, also be argued that humour is used as an 'excuse' for perpetuating certain myths about the ways in which men and women are expected to behave in our society. [10]

Although we live in a society made up of different ethnic groups and different cultures, there is one particular group which tends to dominate television. This imbalance may have appeared to change over the years with the appearance of black newsreaders, presenters, and programmes aimed specifically at a black audience, but British television still finds it very difficult to present a realistic and sympathetic image of other cultures and other races. This is perhaps because audiences have been conditioned into accepting the view that we are one nation and one culture and that this culture is a western one. We therefore find it difficult to accept or understand cultures alien to our own.

Sit-com tends to look at other races and cultures from the viewpoint of the dominant white culture. We therefore get characters such as Alf Garnett in *Till Death Us Do Part* expressing what we are told are the fears and worries of the majority of the population and at the same time being a racist bigot who we are meant to despise. The fact that these negative characteristics were understood as real fears, and he was treated sympathetically by many people who actually agreed with his views, shows how important a vehicle sit-com is for the re-presentation of attitudes and beliefs.

Other programmes from the past which attempted to introduce issues around race, such as *Love Thy Neighbour* or *Mixed Blessings*, also saw these issues from the viewpoint of the dominant white culture. The closer the black families in these sit-coms came to fitting into that culture and society the less of a threat they appeared to present.

More recent sit-coms such as *No Problem* have attempted to present a black 'family' from a black viewpoint, using black writers and a black theatre group to construct the series. The series was aimed predominantly at a black audience, but commercial considerations made it necessary for it to have a broader appeal. It therefore never really managed to present a 'real' picture of black culture to either audience. Black audiences may have enjoyed it because they knew it was not a typical black family. White audiences however may have seen it as a typical black family, thereby confirming their already established ideas and prejudices. (If, for example, viewers of Russian television were to only see programmes such as *Are You Being Served?*, *Hi-De-Hi*, and *The Young Ones* they would get a very odd picture of British society and culture.) What we see as a spoof or joke based around a particular aspect of our culture may be seen by others as typical or normal.[11]

## Narrative and humour

It must be remembered that sit-coms are meant to be funny, and humour is the one thing that separates sit-com from other forms of drama on television, particularly soaps. Sit-com relies on a combination of verbal and visual humour. Verbal humour, being based around the use of language to create jokes or comic situations, allows writers to construct interesting dialogue between characters. Visual humour is particularly appropriate to television because it can select certain images and draw the viewer's attention to them (they include events going on in the scene which the main characters may not see, or going in for a close up of a particular reaction to a joke or event).

In order for sit-com or any other form of comedy to work there must be some kind of 'common experience' to draw upon. A joke about something really obscure would only make a small number of people laugh. In order to appeal to as wide an audience as possible, comedy must draw upon common areas of social and cultural experience which the majority of people are likely to recognize. By doing so it must also exclude large numbers of people whose experiences and perspectives differ from the social and cultural experiences and perspectives of the general majority. Such marginalized groups of people are used as a source of humour, and therefore they do not conform to the majority model. By asserting and assuming a common area of experience and perspective – that of the dominant culture – the diversity of individuals, groups, cultures, beliefs, and attitudes that make up society is rendered invisible. In mirroring the dominance of its ideology in the world outside, sit-com affirms its supremacy and the irrelevance of the offence it may cause. It tends to derive its humour from either our own cultural habits or from those of minority groups. So on the one hand we can find our own eccentricities amusing and on the other we feel safe laughing at people and situations that we choose to define as outside our 'common area of experience'.

But what purpose is the humour actually serving? Clearly one purpose is to make us feel part of a cohesive social group, where we can 'share' a joke. We can also find ourselves laughing at jokes about minority groups whilst recognizing that the joke is actually demeaning to that group. This is partially due to our own social conditioning, and even if we are aware that a joke is racist or sexist we may still respond to it with laughter. The association of people, groups, and cultures with certain characteristics presents us with opinions and stereotypes that, although often false, have been established and absorbed into the consciousness of all cultures.

Sit-coms are not just a collection of unrelated sketches, they follow a narrative structure which has a beginning, middle, and end which follow a logical temporal sequence. The 'story' usually involves some kind of problem or disruption which has to be resolved within the half-hour episode. Some sit-coms may be more fluid or open-ended, and themes may recur throughout the series. Programmes such as *Porridge* or *Hi-De-Hi* may have different incidents in each episode which are sources of humour in the narrative, but overall themes keep recurring. These usually involve the main characters in trying to beat or at least come to terms with the circumstances they find themselves in. We know however that the characters have a set of 'rules' that they follow and these set out certain limits which cannot be crossed. We know for example that Fletcher in *Porridge* and Ted Bovis in *Hi-De-Hi* are 'shady characters', but we also know that they are basically 'good'. This means that they can be relied upon to use humour to assert themselves, but at the same time because they are 'good' we know that situations will eventually be resolved to everyone's advantage.

This link between the main characters and the way in which stories are resolved is very important in sit-com. Because audiences know the characters and the genre, they can predict certain outcomes. We know for example that programmes like *Fawlty Towers* are based around the hopelessness of Basil Fawlty trying to resolve an impossible situation, and a number of episodes end in chaos with the situation not really being effectively resolved.

The narrative structure of sit-com therefore follows a fairly predictable pattern which viewers can relate to and understand. This pattern conforms to certain acceptable definitions of 'realism' which have to be maintained. Sit-coms which step outside these boundaries run the risk of alienating their audience (or in some cases, such as *The Young Ones*, they may attract a particular 'cult' status).

## Conclusion

In popular television drama it is possible to raise issues and explore them through the characters and the situations they find themselves in. However, because sit-com is seen by the television companies as a form of escapist entertainment it becomes more difficult to see the ways in which it may influence its audience. The notion of something that is pleasurable also being of any real importance or value is one that many people may find difficult to accept. If a programme is made purely to entertain without any kind of message for its audience then why shouldn't we just get on and enjoy it? I would argue that if we are prepared to question things that television tells us about the world which are classified as information or news, then why shouldn't we apply the same kind of questioning to entertainment? Television situation comedy, like many other forms of 'popular' television, is far more complex than it first appears, and like any other area of television it is worthy of analysis and critical evaluation.

*Note*: One of the problems of writing about situation comedy is that many comedy series are only broadcast once and unless recorded are unavailable for further study. However, many of the 'classic' sit-coms are now available on video and it seems likely that more will follow. Selected episodes from a number of sit-coms are available for hire from the BFI library (see also note 2 below).

## Notes

1 *The Young Ones*, BBC television: director, Paul Jackson; writers, Ben Elton, Rik Mayall, and Lise Meyer.
2 Cook and North, op. cit. in Further reading.
3 E. Croston (ed.), *Television and Radio 1979 – A Guide to Independent Television and Local Radio*, London: Independent Broadcasting Authority, 1978.
4 Department of Education and Science, *Popular TV and Schoolchildren* London: HMSO, 1983.
5 E. Croston (ed.), *Television and Radio 1982*, London: Independent Broadcasting Authority, 1981.
6 Eaton, op. cit. in Further reading.
7 Andy Medhurst and Lucy Tuck, 'The gender game', in Cook, op. cit. in Further reading. (This is a collection of seven essays about various aspects of sit-com which developed from a BFI summer school on Television Fictions in 1981.)
8 Susan Boyd-Bowman, 'Back to camp', in ibid. and Cary Bazelgette, *Selling Pictures*, London: British Film Institute, 1983.
9 Ben Elton interviewed on *Open to Question*, BBC 2, October 1987.
10 Medhurst and Tuck, op. cit.
11 Paul Gilroy, 'C4 – bridgehead or bantustan?', *Screen*, vol. 24, nos. 4–5 (July–October 1983).

## Further reading

Cook, Jim (ed.), *Television Situation Comedy*, BFI Dossier no. 17, London: British Film Institute, 1982.

Cook, Jim and North, Nicky (eds), *Teaching TV Sitcom*, BFI Education, London: British Film Institute, 1985.

Eaton, Mick, 'Television situation comedy', *Screen*, vol. 19, no. 4 (Winter 1978–9).

Nathan, David, *The Laughtermakers*, London: Peter Owen, 1971.

# 10 TELEVISION AND BLACK BRITONS

## John Tulloch

Modern political crises normally have a media sub-plot. (Jeremy Tunstall)[1]

The debate about broadcasting, from the creation of the British Broadcasting Corporation in the 1920s, has been essentially a debate about the composition and development of the British nation-state. Grossly simplified, the debate has been between those who have seen broadcasting as a form of social engineering – either in the form of new building or maintenance – and those who have argued that broadcasting merely reflects society. For the former, the measure of the system's health has been the degree to which it could meet explicit goals – the fostering of national unity or community spirit, the creation of an informed citizenry, the meeting of educational needs, and so on. For the latter, success has lain in meeting audience demands – expressed variously in the forms of audience figures, profitability, and export success. To a unique extent, therefore, broadcasting has been an arena for the contest between the major political and social groupings in British society.

Broadcasting was born in the aftermath of a total war which accelerated the demise of market forces in the British economy. To survive, the British state was forced to embrace wholesale corporate solutions to the inadequacies of war production. Employers' and workers' organizations became part of an 'extended state' essential for running a war economy. Production targets and the efficient utilization of labour became more important than profitability. For most of the century, this extended state grew by variations on the corporate theme – delegating power to institutions and representative bodies which, although they possessed a varying degree of autonomy and self-management, were in reality senior or junior partners in the running of the country.

This corporate climate was profoundly hostile to the workings of a market economy. Nowhere was this more clearly to be seen than in broadcasting. The BBC was set up in response to the conflicting demands of the radio industry, the Post Office, the armed services, and the newspaper industry, as a monopoly susceptible to control by the state. Broadcasting was seen primarily as a threat, rather than an opportunity – a source of enormous, if unknown power which must be tightly controlled. The audience was seen as essentially passive and malleable. The BBC's first Director-General, John Reith, gave single-minded utterance to this corporate view of consumers: 'It is occasionally indicated to us that we are apparently setting out to give the public what we think they need – and not what they want – but few know what they want and very few what they need.'[2]

In the interwar period of unchallenged BBC monopoly, the Post Office and the corporation combined to exclude any competition from other services, fettering the development of cable and effectively forcing competition abroad; in the late 1930s, commercial radio stations like Radios Normandie or Luxembourg, operating from the continent, became increasingly popular with British working-class listeners, bored with the middle-class diet provided by the BBC. The climate of corporatism created among broadcasters a sense that they had been entrusted with a special mission to elevate their audience. They were the 'new priesthood'. Typical of this cast of mind was the BBC's Director-General, William Haley (1946–52) who wrote that broadcasting 'should play its part in bringing about the reign of truth' and that because society was composed of competing intolerant groups broadcasting could 'only be left to those in charge of broadcasting'.[3]

The 'Reithian' ethos was of course much larger than the narrow vision of a Reith or a Haley. Tom Burns has written most perceptively of the character of 'BBC culture':

> The BBC was developed under Reith into a kind of domestic diplomatic service, representing the British – or what he saw as the best of the British – to the British. BBC culture, like BBC standard English, was not peculiar to itself but an intellectual ambience composed out of the values, ¨tandards and beliefs of the professional

middle class, especially that part educated at Oxford and Cambridge. Sports, popular music and entertainment which appealed to the lower classes were included in large measure in the programmes, but the manner in which they were purveyed, the context and the presentation, remained indomitably upper middle class; and there was, too, the point that they were only there on the menu as ground bait.[4]

The corporate bias in the management of the state, which the BBC exemplified, succeeded for forty years in playing down class conflict and creating a broad political consensus in economic and social policy. This consensus began to dissolve in the 1960s. Commercial television destroyed the BBC's monopoly and introduced new models of pro-gramming to the public, although it was itself established within a regulatory framework operated by the ITA that owed much to the corporate ideology of public service broadcasting. Competition forced the BBC into a high-risk strategy of dissent under the director-generalship of Sir Hugh Greene, who encouraged a vast expansion of broadcast journalism, 'kitchen sink' drama, and – most notoriously – political satire.

Forced to remodel its services under the impact of commercial television, the BBC also faced the competition of 'pirate radio' in the early 1960s, with offshore stations developing large audiences of young working-class listeners. Although the government stepped in to ban it, the BBC was forced to remodel its radio services – creating Radios 1 and 2 – and dust off plans for a nationwide system of 'local' radio stations.

'Local' radio, 'community' politics, 'public participation' in planning – in retrospect, broadcasting can be seen to reflect a general process of social tinkering in the 1960s that was the corporate response to the realities of relative economic decline and the increasingly intractable problems of a nation that could not foreseeably meet the basic needs – jobs, homes, reasonable security – of large social groups. This was the background to the emergence of 'ethnic minorities' and 'race relations' as a 'problem' not only for the state but for the broadcasters. What could corporatism do for black Britons?

## The black 'problem'

I don't think the authorities realised that the name Black Londoners would last, otherwise they might not have allowed it. . . . I would

143

listen to them saying 'If only Alex could find a different name for the programme.' (Alex Pascall, producer of BBC Radio London's *Black Londoners*)[5]

Before the black immigration of the 1950s and 1960s, broadcasting had mainly presented black people as 'foreigners'. It is instructive to recall that 'even after Britain had acquired a substantial domestic black population. . .the single most regular exposure of 'black' people on the television screen was *The Black and White Minstrel Show*'.[6] Subsequently the typical presentation of blacks was as 'problems', as the pressures created by unequal treatment in the field of employment, housing, and law and order led to communal friction and finally wholesale conflict on the streets. Governments in the 1960s attempted to contain these conflicts by a dual policy – enacting ever more stringent and racist immigration controls and preaching a consensus policy of good race relations at home.

A series of measures starting with the passage of the first Commonwealth Immigration Bill in 1962 effectively institutionalized racism and set the agenda for media presentation of the issue. Press coverage both reflected this policy and helped to articulate popular racism, in a complex exchange best summarized by Gideon Ben-Tovim and John Gabriel:

> Perhaps it would be most accurate to see the popular articulation of racist exclusivism and the enactment of racist policies as a dialectical process, an interchange between politicians and people within structurally determinant but also very fluent conditions in which the media have played an important role as lightning-conductor of the most negative definitions and reactions from both sources.[7]

In a survey of every thirteenth copy of *The Times*, *Guardian*, *Daily Mirror*, and *Daily Express* from 1963 to 1970, Hartmann *et al.* found that certain key themes in the coverage were shared by all four newspapers, despite their political differences. These were: immigration control measures, the level of immigration itself, black/white relations, and the pronouncements and doings of Enoch Powell. They argue that the agenda for debate that was set was a simple one – 'Keeping the blacks out.'[8]

In contrast to the press, broadcasting maintained through the 1960s a more cautious attitude to the reporting of race issues. The first 'ethnic minority' programmes were launched in 1965 after conferences with West Indian and Asian organizations, and the new local radio system was given the task of providing a range of minority programmes.

144

The BBC's attitude on the reporting of racism was robust, with Sir Hugh Greene trenchantly stating:

> In talking about the BBC's obligation to be impartial I ought to make it clear that we are not impartial about everything. There are, for instance, two very important exceptions. We are not impartial about crime. . .nor are we impartial about race hatred.[9]

The watershed for both press and broadcasting was Enoch Powell's 1968 'river of blood' speech in Birmingham, which shocked the political establishment by the groundswell of white, racist support that was evoked. So intense was the coverage that a Gallup poll found that knowledge of the speech had reached 96 per cent of the adult population a few days later. As Colin Seymour-Ure has commented:

> The effect of Powell's speech was to convince those media controllers who required convincing that any special responsibility to avoid worsening or inflaming a delicate situation, which had often led them in the past to suspend or downgrade normal news values, was now clearly outweighed by the need to keep public confidence.[10]

Powell's 'earthquake' had the effect of opening up the public debate about race and forcing corporate managers to register the reality of white racism and reluctantly introduce more active policies. But for the news media blackness became linked to internal conflict – a conflict that had to be contained.

As British blacks began to establish community and self-help organizations in the face of white racism their pressure increased on the corporate managers of British broadcasting for programmes and coverage which reflected their own needs and experience – through demands for access to television and radio programming and for equal opportunities in broadcasting employment. One area of conflict was in the BBC's local radio stations.

The BBC's local radio stations were launched in the late 1960s with the claim that they would produce a grassroots service which would complement the national pattern of network and regional radio. Local radio's proponents envisaged the new services as having a community building function. But what community? The elastic, cosy concept of bringing people in a locality together was at odds with the real processes by which the aspirations of those outside the magic circle of the consensus with serious demands to make of the majority might be voiced. The whole previous framework of British broadcasting had been designed to contain and control the 'right to broadcast' to recognized groups who posed no threat to the majority. In the case of *Black Londoners* – a test bed for 'ethnic minority' programming – the forging of a black audience had serious political implications and created problems for white managers.

Although *Black Londoners* survived it remained underfunded – until October 1988 when Radio London was superseded by GLR – and reliant on the work of largely unpaid freelances. It faced the same contradictions experienced by community organizations. Working on *Black Londoners* or many of the 'ethnic minority' programmes that now exist has not led to representation on management structures or increased employment for black journalists in the newsroom or 'mainstream' production jobs. While ethnic minority broadcasting has provided a token that stations are 'doing something' about race they have tended to be employment ghettos for the young, often unpaid, blacks involved.

### 'Invisible' broadcasters

Research on the role of ethnic minorities in broadcasting shares one overwhelming finding – there is broad agreement that, with a few exceptions, black people are simply *absent* as performers, journalists and production workers. Nailing down the real dimensions of this absence has proved difficult – broadcasting organizations have resisted an open process of ethnic monitoring because the fear that hard information would provide a basis for demands for quotas or targets of black employees. However, some research has been done on broadcast output by the Commission for Racial Equality, which has undertaken a number of monitoring studies in recent years. One study, which monitored television output for six weeks in 1978–9, found that, in drama, white UK and US actors accounted for an average of 78 per cent of appearances, West Indians for 5 per cent, and Asians for 1 per cent.

The study concluded that the frequency of appearances by ethnic minority performers was generally low.

> Although West Indians appear more frequently, and in a greater variety of roles than other ethnic minorities, the same cannot be said for Indians, Pakistanis and other Asian minorities. Asian minorities appear most frequently in current affairs programmes, children's programmes and light entertainment such as comedy series. However, the majority of such appearances are merely as background. As far as Asians and black African roles are concerned, there appears little evidence of any serious attempt to cover the range of occupations and activities involving these groups in society.[11]

146

Although a later CRE study monitoring output for 1983–4 found significant improvements, the overall figures for appearances still remained low.

No similar monitoring study has been undertaken for news output but the impression that there are still few black journalists or producers working in broadcasting – while those that do are concentrated in ethnic minority programmes like the BBC's *Ebony* or Channel 4's *The Bandung File* – is borne out by other information. The National Union of Journalists estimates that only around 300 of its 34,000 members are black and has recently started to monitor all new members. A register of black media workers compiled a few years ago listed less than 300 people.

Why are black people underrepresented in the broadcast media? The CRE links several factors. The black perception that the media is largely a white preserve discourages young blacks from seeking careers in journalism, acting, or production work. The Commission also points to a lack of education and training opportunities for young blacks, already disadvantaged by the school system. A third factor is the ignorance and/or racism of white employers. For example, the CRE study found that the main reason given by producers for the lack of black actors was that the type of programmes produced made it inappropriate to cast them. It was argued that black actors had little or no place in most costume or period drama – a staple of television production – ignoring the fact that England and Wales had a substantial black presence (up to 20,000 in London) concentrated in major ports by the mid-eighteenth century. But the study also found that one in five producers questioned also identified 'quality of actors' as a reason for not casting blacks.

The CRE research sees a link between the lack of jobs available to black performers and their representation:

> The portrayal of ethnic minorities in Drama, Light Entertainment and other programme areas depends to a large extent on the employment opportunities open to ethnic minority artists. Any difficulties they face will have a two-fold effect: first on employment prospects, secondly on the 'visibility' and roles which television gives to those of ethnic minority origin.[12]

Despite the advent of Channel 4 and more adventurous policies in commissioning drama (such as *The Chinese Detective*) by the BBC and some independent companies, the CRE's research indicates that 'the roles and situations in which [blacks] are presented serve to reinforce existing stereotypes'. These stereotypes operate in two ways – by confining black performers to obviously 'black' background roles such as singers, bus conductors, servants, and so on, and by linking black performers to obvious 'conflict' or 'problem' areas.

As long ago as 1969 the actors' union Equity adopted a policy of 'integrated casting' – that is, the casting of performers on the basis of their ability as performers regardless of their colour. In 1983 Equity was still pushing for positive moves towards this goal but found that progress had – in the words of its President – been 'appallingly slow'.

Britain's major soap operas – with the notable exception of the BBC's *EastEnders* – are still reluctant to cast black characters in 'normal' situations. This problem was discussed in a 1983 Equity report:

> The first thing that was discussed in our [working] group was the introduction of a black family in *Coronation Street*. The group said, in view of the fact that one of the programme planners of Granada had said that this was impossible without a conflict situation arising in the plot, that approaches should be made to the Management, Directors and even the cast to see if they are of the same opinion. . . . If they really want to depict a street in Manchester, reality would require the inclusion of a black family.[13]

Two arguments are embedded here. One is that broadcasting, by its failure to employ blacks, does not adequately reflect the 'reality' of British society. But the second is that a 'positive image' will help to virtuously transform those realities – which include racism and mass black unemployment – by influencing the attitudes of the white audience to see blacks positively while enhancing black self-esteem.

A similar set of arguments has been applied to the news media by the CRE and the broadcasting unions. The pressure here has been for the recruitment and training of more black journalists and producers to at least reflect the 4 per cent of blacks in the British population and the 15 per cent in areas like London. But the point is also made that black representation will increase the credibility of the news and current affairs output for the black audience: a similar argument to that made for the recruitment of black police.

Colleges and employers have recently launched a number of initiatives to recruit and train more black journalists. Both the BBC and Channel 4 started training courses for black broadcasters in 1987, while BBC local radio has also recruited black applicants for news training in the last three years. A positive action course in broadcast journalism has been run successfully at the Polytechnic of Central London since 1983 and at least 60 per cent of graduates have found full-time jobs in broadcasting. Other colleges – notably Vauxhall College in London – have also set up positive action courses, while the NUJ started a special scholarship scheme to finance black trainees on journalism courses in 1987.

But neither the BBC or Channel 4 schemes embody a continuing commitment to black training and they are limited to roughly eighteen recruits. The PCL intake is limited to twelve students and is dependent on year-on-year MSC finance. On the NUJ figures alone, current initiatives could take up to thirty years to make good the shortage of black broadcasters and journalists.

## Finding acceptable stereotypes?

When we reflect society as it is – with all its prevailing class, sex and racial bigotry – we are accused of pandering to ignorance. But when we attempt to challenge stereotypes, we are accused of peddling fantasy, not reality.[14]

The objective of proponents of 'integrated casting' is for greater black representation in broadcast fiction and news programmes with a range, not of black characters, but characters who happen to be black. There is little doubt that some broadcasting executives now display much greater sensitivity to the issues of black representation and this has been reflected in a number of recent one-off plays and drama serials dealing with the relationships both within minority groups and between different groups. Recent examples are Channel 4's multicultural situation comedy *The Desmonds*, BBC 2's *Shalom Salaam*, a drama serial based on relationships between different ethnic groups, and several other instances. Channel 4 has also taken the lead in commissioning highly successful feature film treatments of such themes, for example *Sammy and Rosie Get Laid* and *My Beautiful Laundrette*.

However, there is still a distinct lack of what might be described as run-of-the-mill black characters. Producers can reasonably argue that, given the perceptible lack of black lawyers, senior police officers, and managers in British society itself, it is stretching audience credibility (and perhaps using the medium as a propaganda vehicle for an establishment committed to denying the facts of racial disadvantage) to populate the screen with black characters in elite roles and make no dramatic exploitation of their ethnicity.

But there have been notable exceptions. Thames TV has cast a black police officer in its drama series *The Bill*, for example. While his ethnicity is an issue at times in the series it has figured less than the dramatic situations created by an inexperienced officer learning the job, fitting in with colleagues. A similar approach was taken in the recent drama series on the London Fire Brigade, *London's Burning*. A number of characters in the BBC's drama serial *EastEnders* are black, and although previous members of the cast have achieved coverage in the tabloid press on the 'Why I am Leaving *EastEnders*' theme there has been a consistent policy of using black characters in a variety of roles. However, black characters are most notably absent from that actor's staple, television advertising. 'British admen today tend to avoid any accusations of Caucasian-inspired racism by the simple device of excluding black faces from commercials wherever possible.'[15]

### The limits of corporatism

Corporatism breeds its own special temper of mind – that of the 'platonic guardian' – and if it is expressed in more tentative tones nowadays than in the time of Reith, it remains a persistent feature of the corporate view of the world:

> The Chairman of the IBA, when innocently asked in 1982 by an eminent Canadian communication scholar, 'How do you decide what is in the public interest?' replied, 'I have been appointed to this office because I know what the public interest is.[16]

In the corporate model the viewer or listener is essentially a passive and potentially vulnerable consumer. S/he must be protected as well as informed, educated, and entertained. S/he may even be led to higher things as in Sir William Haley's classic formulation of the community receiving network radio as 'a broadly based cultural pyramid slowly aspiring upwards' from the Light Programme to the Home Service to the Third Programme.[17] But what cannot be conceded is that control or accountability should move away from the 'in-group' of professionals. Although black community organizations and to some extent the CRE have been in a position to extract some concessions from the corporate system – in terms of ethnic minority programming and moves towards positive action in recruitment and training – the real gains, after twenty years of negotiation, have been small compared to the achievement of US blacks in wresting concessions on integrated casting and job recruitment. As David Milner notes:

> It is only within the last ten years that the [US] networks have taken at all seriously the demands for greater and better representation of minorities in programming. Before this time the medium was almost exclusively white, the tiny proportion of programmes which included

black characters portraying them as happy-go-lucky, unreliable 'coons', maids and manservants, entertainers and athletes.[18]

The reason for the change lies partly in skilful political lobbying and the election of a wide range of black political representatives. But this has been founded on the emergence of a black audience with a numerically large middle-class elite able to exert real economic pressure on the US broadcasting system. Although British blacks are numerically a smaller proportion of the population and vastly less prosperous, the creation of minority programming and an ethnic press shows the beginnings of the emergence of a black audience. How can its demands be met?

Peacock embraced a model of the consumer very different to that envisaged by corporatism. His consumer is no passive, vulnerable audience member but a robust individual able to make choices and exert preferences. The main finding of the Peacock Report was therefore that

> British broadcasting should move towards a sophisticated market system based on consumer sovereignty. This is a system which recognises that viewers and listeners are the best ultimate judges of their own interests, which they can best satisfy if they have the option of purchasing the broadcasting services they require from as many alternative sources of supply as possible.[19]

The report laid out a three-stage plan for creating a broadcasting market with a requirement of freedom of entry for programme makers, a transmission system capable of carrying an indefinitely large range of programmes, and facilities for paying for programmes or particular services. But its interim proposal – a first stage towards the creation of a market – is of more immediate interest to British blacks.

> One way of introducing competition, even while the duopoly remains, is by enlarging the scope of independent programme makers to sell to existing authorities, as already occurs in the case of Channel 4. The three functions of making programmes, packaging them into channels, and delivering them to the viewer or listener are distinct; and it is mainly a historical accident that links them together.

The report therefore recommended that the BBC and ITV should be required over a ten-year period to increase to not less than 40 per cent the proportion of programmes supplied by independent producers.

While Peacock's notion of the 'sovereign' consumer is difficult for corporate power-holders – and the Conservative government, ironically – to accept, it is one that holds out real prospects of new and radical change for the 'outsiders' in the present system. As the largest group of outsiders in British broadcasting, blacks have little to lose and much to gain from exerting substantial pressure for a presence in the new broadcasting market that is representative of their numbers.

## Notes

1 Jeremy Tunstall, *The Media in Britain*, London: Constable, 1983.
2 John Reith, *Broadcast Over Britain*, London: Hodder & Stoughton, 1924.
3 Quoted in Michael Tracey, *A Variety of Lives: A Biography of Sir Hugh Greene*, London: Bodley Head, 1983.
4 Tom Burns, *The BBC: Public Institution and Private World*, London: Macmillan, 1977.
5 Quoted in Phil Cohen, op. cit. in Further reading
6 David Milner, *Children and Race Ten Years On*, London: Ward Lock, 1983.
7 Gideon Ben-Tovim and John Gabriel, 'The politics of race in Britain, 1962–1979', in Charles Husband (ed.), *Race In Britain*, London: Hutchinson, 1982.
8 Paul Hartman *et al.*, *Race as News*, Paris: UNESCO, 1974.
9 Sir Hugh Greene, quoted in Braham, op. cit. in Further reading.
10 Colin Seymore-Ure, *The Political Impact of the Mass Media*, London: Constable, 1974.
11 Muhammad Anwar and Anthony Shang, *Television in a Multiracial Society*, London: Commission for Racial Equality, 1982.
12 ibid.
13 *Report on the Conference on Integrated Casting*, London: British Actors Equity Association, 1983.
14 Virginia Matthews, 'Race for money', *Listener*, 23 February 1989.
15 ibid.
16 Quoted in Richard Collins, Nicholas Garnham, and Gareth Locksley, *The Economics of Television: The UK Case*, London: Sage, 1988.
17 Sir William Haley, 'The Lewis Fry Memorial Lecture', in Anthony Smith (ed.), *British Broadcasting*, Newton Abbot: David & Charles, 1974.
18 Milner, op. cit.
19 Peacock Committee, *Report of the Committee on Financing the BBC* (The Peacock Report), Cmnd. 9824, London: HMSO, 1986.

## Further reading

Braham, Peter, 'How the media report race', in Michael Gurevitch *et al.* (eds), *Culture, Society and the Media*, London: Methuen, 1982.
Cohen, Phil (ed.), *It Ain't Half Racist, Mum*, London: Comedia, 1982.
Gilroy, Paul, *There Ain't No Black in the Union Jack*, London: Hutchinson, 1987.
Husband, Charles, *White Media and Black Britain*, London: Hutchinson, 1975.

# 11 ARE YOU RECEIVING ME?

*Justin Lewis*

Television today represents one of the most important sources ·of information available to our society. Hours upon hours of words and images flood from the TV screen into most people's homes every day. It has become part of our environment, as varied or repetitive as the jobs some of us do when we are not watching it. It teaches us, tells stories, makes us laugh, makes us angry – it guides us into a whole series of different worlds and asks us to position ourselves in relation to them.

There is no shortage of research attempting to understand the nature and significance of this extraordinary cultural phenomenon. In spite of this, television has grown to an extent beyond our current ability to comprehend and analyse its power and influence. Social scientists have, since the popular use of the TV set, been preoccupied with particular questions about it. That is fair enough. What has been less fortunate is the preoccupation with certain ways of answering those questions.

## The effect of television

The first identifiable set of questions about television failed to produce any decisive results. These questions came from within a body of research that has become known, for obvious reasons, as the 'effects' approach. This approach attempted to address a fundamental and very general question: what effect does television have on people? The scope for investigation opened up by such a question is clearly enormous, so it was not surprising that researchers limited themselves to specific kinds of 'effect' and used a specific set of investigative tools. The most popular fields of inquiry were the effects of (political) television on political attitudes and the question of whether violence on the screen precipitated violent behaviour. There is, of course, nothing wrong with these questions. The problems with the 'effects' approach are problems of method.

If you want to measure the effect of hitting people on the head with a hammer, it is not going to be difficult to come up with a workable methodology for doing so. We can, on the basis of a vast body of accumulated evidence, anticipate a range of immediate responses: the person hit on the head is likely to howl with pain, fall over, or drop down dead. However, supposing we want to measure long-term effects (if the unfortunate subject of the research lives that long) we can both anticipate them (whether mental or physical) and devise ways of measuring them. This is because:

  (i) we can locate a clear difference between those who have recently been hit on the head and those who have not;
 (ii) we can look for a range of possible reactions;
(iii) we can monitor a specific group of people to see whether these reactions occur;
(iv) this group can easily be composed of people who have not been hit on the head;
 (v) intervening variables (like being hit on the head again) can be easily isolated, recorded, and assimilated into the monitoring process.

Watching television may sometimes *feel* like being hit on the head, but its effects are much more difficult to measure. The 'effects' tradition of research failed fully to appreciate the subtleties of this. If we want to find out whether, say, TV makes people more violent or changes their politics, we are confronted by complications at almost every stage.

1 Watching television embraces a multitude of sins. We may chat, eat our tea, or do the ironing while watching. A programme may be interspersed with comments from members of the family, or it may be watched in total silence. Moreover, since we know that the TV world and the real world are not the same, we don't necessarily perceive TV violence and real violence as having much to do with each other.
2 Because so many people are exposed to so much television, it is extremely difficult to isolate particular kinds of exposure. It is difficult, for example, to divide people into those who have watched a lot of violence on TV since the age of five and those who have not.

154

3 Even if we were able to make distinctions between people on the basis of which programmes they watch, this begs a number of questions. People who, for example, watch violent TV programmes may do so for a number of specific reasons. These primary motivations may be far more important than the programmes they watch as a result. Any differences which then emerge between the people who watch violent programmes and people who don't may, therefore, have nothing to do with viewing habits at all. Watching TV could be a product of the same influences that make people violent. So, even if we were able to isolate a group of people who watched a lot of violence on TV, and even if we were able to show that those people were more likely to behave violently, we could not prove that one caused the other.

4 The problem of isolating causes and effects raises the much bigger questions of *ideology*. Television is what Louis Althusser would call an 'ideological apparatus'. In other words, it is a set of meaning systems that will influence the way we think about the world. It is, however, just one of many: the family, the school, the press – all these are ideological apparatuses that shape the way we think. These ideological influences intermingle throughout our daily lives, reacting with us as social beings. Any attempt to analyse social and ideological agencies has to take account of other agencies that may intervene.

These problems are, of course, common to all types of audience research, not just the 'effects' approach. The 'effects' tradition was, on the whole, particularly unsuccessful at overcoming them precisely because television viewing was analysed as if it *was* a hammer hitting people on the head. The ubiquitous nature of TV viewing in a complex ideological world often made 'effects' studies either ambiguous or unsuccessful. So 'effects' research repeatedly, over the years, proved and disproved, for example, that violence on television makes people violent.

The fact that 'effects' studies failed to yield positive results had more to do with the limits of the methodology than with television's lack of power and influence. Carl Hovland, writing in 1959, pointed out that 'effects' research was frequently not capable of answering the questions it posed, because of the investigative methods used.[1] Reviewing the media research of the period, he demonstrated that the conflicting results they produced could be traced back to the way the research was done. Briefly, those surveys which were able to measure controlled exposure to media (before and after exposure) yielded more positive results than those sample surveys that simply attempted to draw correlations between exposure and attitude where 'before and after' controls are difficult or impossible.

Typical of the latter was Blumler and McQuail's work on the 1959 British general election, which concluded that: 'Within the frame of reference set up by our experiment, political change was neither related to the degree of exposure nor to any particular programme or argument put forward by the parties'.[2] This conclusion is not all that surprising. The complex set of ideological forces that create or change a person's political outlook are unlikely to be dislodged by a single medium in three weeks. Such a conclusion is, however, profoundly misleading. It suggests that television does not influence people's political attitudes (a finding in line with preceding 'effects' studies of political attitudes). There are three specific problems here.

First, the long-term influence of television is neglected. While television *may* be capable of inspiring fairly rapid changes in attitude, its more profound influence will be more subtle and gradual. As Gillian Dyer points out when writing about the influence of advertising:

> It is more than likely that an advertisement's effects are diffuse and long term, and there is some evidence that advertising plays a part in defining 'reality' in a general or anthropological sense . . . for instance, the sex-role stereotyping common to many advertisements – the 'little woman' as household functionary thrilling to her new polished table or whiter-than-white sheets, or the masterful, adventurous male – act, many social scientists argue, as agents of socialisation and lead many people, young and old, to believe in traditional and discriminatory sex roles.[3]

Secondly, for television to have a *measurable* short-term effect, other media or ideological agencies will have to be silent. If TV viewers and non-TV viewers behave the same way during an election campaign, this may demonstrate that television *is* influencing attitudes but that it is working in the same way as other agencies (like the press).

Studies that have isolated particular types of media effect have shown far more movement. Hartmann and Husband's study of racist attitudes, for example, found that the media played a significant role in building up racist attitudes, images, and stereotypes in all-white areas.[4] Quite simply the media was the only major source of information available to people on this subject.

Thirdly, the 'effect' of television will not necessarily be unitary. A series of news broadcasts could have a profound influence on people without necessarily influencing them *in the same way*. Television programmes are complex collections of words and images. The meanings we construct from these words and images will depend on our positions in the world and the view we take of it.

This final point suggests an approach that acknowledges the viewer as an active subject, selecting and interpreting what she or he watches. It is to just such an approach I now turn.

## Uses and gratifications

The failure of most studies to demonstrate television's effects unambiguously led social scientists to become disenchanted with the questions being asked, and to search for new questions within new frameworks. Thus began 'the functional approach to the media, or the "uses and gratifications" approach. It is the program that asks the question not "what do the media do to people" but, "what do people do with the media?"'.[5]

This change in direction shifted power away from the television screen towards the viewer, who used television to gratify certain needs. As McQuail, Blumler, and Brown put it: 'Our model of this process is that of an open system in which social experience gives rise to certain needs, some of which are directed to the mass media of communication for satisfaction'.[6] The 'uses and gratifications' approach was extremely influential, in both Britain and the United States, from the 1950s to the 1970s. It liberated the viewer from a supposed role as the passive recipient of television messages, providing space for a more sophisticated analysis of the viewing process.

In some ways, this was clearly a theoretical advance. The 'uses and gratifications' approach did, however, raise problems as well as solve them. There is a sense in which the baby had been thrown out with the bathwater. As I have already indicated, underlying the 'effects' approach were perfectly legitimate questions about the influence of television on the way we think and behave. The problem with the 'effects' research was its simplistic view of the whole process of TV viewing, which was placed inside an ideological vacuum. The ideological world that the viewer inhabited was too complex to be absorbed into the 'hammer on the head' approach of 'effects' research. The 'uses and gratifications' approach, in asserting the viewer's power to select and interpret, abandoned not only the 'effects' methodology, but the questions that that methodology failed to answer.

Television, in this perspective, becomes merely a source of 'gratification' for the viewer, whose power to select and interpret appears to reduce its ideological force almost to vanishing point. Television is the most dominant source of information in our society, occupying us for an average of 20 hours per week. To understand it as a purely functional entity is like equating sex and sexuality with the moment of orgasm.

At the heart of the problems raised by 'uses and gratifications' is its introduction of a social world which it does not fully understand. The notion of ideology is introduced, only to be displaced by the idea of 'use' or motivation. This was succinctly revealed by Elihu Katz, when he wrote that: 'The uses approach assumes that people's values, their interests, their associations, their social roles, are preponderent and that people selectively "fashion" what they see and hear to those interests'.[7] This brings in the idea that the viewer is a social being, a carrier of ideologies – 'values . . . interests . . . associations . . . social roles' – on the one hand, while reducing these ideas to a set of motivations on the other.

The limitations of this approach were revealed in another election study by Blumler and McQuail. Having failed to find any positive results using the 'effects' approach in 1959, their next attempt incorporated 'uses and gratifications'. This appeared to be more successful, demonstrating that certain groups of voters responded differently to party political broadcasts. Their use of the 'uses and gratifications' perspective led them to conclude that:

> the strongly motivated voters had responded in one direction and the less keen in another . . . whereas opinions of the strongly motivated voters were influenced by major party propaganda, the politically less keen electors responded favourably to the presentation of the Liberal case.[8]

Put in this way, the difference between the readings and responses of the 'less keen' and 'strongly motivated' are extremely difficult to explain. The problem here is the idea of motivation. Blumler and McQuail use the concept because it fits the 'uses and gratifications' model, but what does it actually mean?

If we substitute 'motivation' with 'ideology', these differences become explicable. The 'strongly motivated' groups were defined as such because they thought within a certain ideological viewpoint. The 'weakly motivated' viewers, on the other hand, clearly did not have the ideologies necessary to respond positively to the Conservative or Labour broadcasts. The Liberal broadcasts, however, did not require these ideologies (or required a different set of perspectives) for viewers to respond positively. It may be, for example, that the Labour and Conservative broadcasts worked within a framework of traditional parliamentary issues (like 'balance of payments'). This approach would attract those people who were familiar with those political ideas and alienate those who were not.

Where does that leave us? The limitations of 'effects' and 'uses and gratifications', once understood, provide the conditions for developing a more sophisticated approach. Such an approach must take into account the nature of television as an ideological apparatus and the fact that our view of the world is shaped by this and other apparatuses. Watching TV therefore becomes a complex interplay of ideologies.

## The meaning of television

In Britain in the 1970s, approaches that had been developed in literary theory, psychoanalysis, and social theory began to be applied to media studies. These new approaches shifted the focus of media research not only away from 'effects' and 'uses and gratifications' but from audience studies generally. The emphasis moved towards the *message* of television, what it said and how it said it. On one level, the idea that television was socially or politically 'neutral' or 'impartial' was challenged – notably by the Glasgow University Media Group in their *Bad News* studies. On the other, the content of television was analysed as a socially conducted set of meanings. These meanings were broken down and scrutinized in journals like *Screen* and *Screen Education*, or related to social and ideological processes in studies like *Policing the Crisis* (Hall *et al.*).

In many ways, this shift towards the TV programme or programmes was both important and useful. Sophisticated forms of analysis from semiology, cultural studies, textual analysis, and ideology were applied and developed in relation to television. These developments have significantly increased our understanding of various forms of television and how they work.

One of the most important of these developments was the application of semiotics to television. Semiotics is the study of meaning – what meanings are attached to things, why those meanings are attached, and how they are attached. Here, at last, was a method for developing TV audience research.

The first principle of semiotics is that there is no natural relation between a thing (whether that thing is a sound, an image, or the kitchen table) and the meaning of that thing (the concepts we use to understand it). Rather, this meaning is seen as the product of our relationship with the thing, of our position in the world, and the ideologies that enable us to understand it. So, for example, when we see a number of men on our screens dressed in white scattered around a comparatively empty but

159

substantial green space, while simultaneously hearing a voice that does not appear to originate from anywhere on the picture, most of us would be able to say that we were watching a game of cricket. This understanding comes from a whole series of ideologies – or, to be more specific, from various *cultural codes*.

Some of these codes will have been learnt at home and at school – codes that allow us to understand what a 'game' or 'sport' is, for example. To a visitor from another planet who had no notion of games or sport, watching a cricket match or a baseball game would be like witnessing a weird and incomprehensible ritual. To most of the non-cricket-playing world on this planet, watching a cricket match would be comprehensible in terms of a *general* cultural code about sport, but only a very specific cultural code – the rules of cricket – would enable them to understand fully what was going on.

Watching a cricket match on TV would only become fully clear, however, if the viewer had the complex cultural codes for understanding television. The mysterious voice from somewhere out of the picture we are able, as well-trained TV watchers, to understand as the voice of 'a commentator'. The fact that the men in white appear and disappear quite suddenly, simultaneously growing or shrinking, does not contravene the laws of science. To the trained viewer, such abnormalities appear quite natural – we *know* that TV broadcasts can switch from one camera to another, from one lens to another, and we are *used* to seeing it that way.

Watching TV, in short, requires learning and skill. We need to learn both the codes or rules of the world it communicates and the codes/rules of the way it communicates them.

In semiotics, this process of constructing meaning is called *signification*. This is the process where the 'thing' or signifier (the picture of a cricket match, for example) we see, hear, or experience is interpreted. This interpretation is not natural but learnt – it involves attaching a concept – or signified – (like 'cricket is a sport') to that 'thing'. The interpreted – or signified – 'thing' is called a *sign*. In short: the signifier (thing) + the signified (concept) = the sign.

Once we have come to terms with this new terminology, the process it describes seems perfectly obvious. What, then, have we gained simply by describing it with a new set of words?

The answer lies in the assertion that, to stress it once more, the relation between signifier and signified is not *natural* but *learnt*. Objects, images, sounds, smells do not naturally mean anything. A picture of Prince Charles could signify any number of things: wealth, royalty, the ruling class, a white man, husband of Princess Diana, English imperialism, and so on and so on. A second picture of Prince Charles talking to a Rastafarian in Brixton may, depending on the first association and a whole range of new ones, signify class difference, racial conflict, racial harmony, cultural imperialism, or simply 'what a nice man of the people Prince Charles is'.

It is the *ambiguity* of the process of signification that makes it so important to define it and understand it as precisely as possible. It is in this sense that we can talk about 'cultural codes'. The way we construct meanings will depend on the cultural codes we have learnt. This, in turn, will depend on our material circumstances – the kind of society we live in, our position in it, family, school – the whole range of our experience. · To make sense of television's multifarious and complex words and images is, effectively, to *decode* them. To study the influence or role of television on people is, therefore, to study a *process of decoding*.

This clearly takes us a long way from 'effects' and 'uses and gratifications'. In the 1970s, however, it was purely a theoretical advance. While knowledge of the *process* of decoding became more sophisticated, attempts to use this knowledge for decoding audience research were few and far between. The sheer complexity of the task created a gaping hole in our knowledge, described by John Hartley thus:

> The growing areas of semiotics and communication studies developed largely out of textual analysis of various kinds . . . and as a result, there is currently a gap in research into social discourses like the news. Most of what happens when the text is 'realised' as a 'live' discourse, when it is read by the consumer is a mystery. As Patrick Moore says about other mysteries of the cosmos, 'we just don't know'.[9]

It is this gap that we need to fill if we are to begin really to understand the possible effects of television. It is into this gap that this research falls, as an attempt to begin to solve the 'mystery' of 'what happens when the text is . . . read by the consumer', to investigate the precise relation between the message and the way that message is read.

## The television experience

The trouble is, of course, that research into the meanings generated by TV viewing is extraordinarily difficult to carry out. We cannot sit inside people heads as they settle down to *Dallas* or *The News at Ten*. This, combined with dwindling budgets for research and the technological distractions of video, cable, and satellite, has limited the development of TV audience research.

Despite this, the 1980s have seen some practical developments within a new, more sophisticated framework. These developments have attempted to avoid assumptions about what particular programmes might mean or the way we respond to them, using in-depth, relatively unstructured interviews with people as a way of reconstructing the experience of watching TV.

It is unusual to be able to pinpoint clearly the beginning of a research 'tradition' (a word it is still perhaps a little too early to use). In this instance, however, David Morley's book *The Nationwide Audience*, published in 1980, represents just such a landmark. Set within the context of semiotics and cultural studies, Morley's study involves a wide range of in-depth interviews with groups following the watching of a video recording of a (then) recent current affairs programme, *Nationwide*. Morley prompted the various groups to construct their own 'decodings' of the programme, before analysing why a group of, say, working-class young women should have come up with one set of meanings and a group of trainee lab technicians with another. The original intention was to see how people's social class determined the meanings they gave to the programme. What the research in fact revealed was a much more specific set of influences, based on the 'discourses' available to people, be they a mainstream working class populism, trade union and labour party politics, or the influence of black youth cultures (Morley 1980: 137).

My own research on decoding *The News at Ten* attempted to develop this discovery (Lewis 1985). A detailed analysis of viewers' reconstructions and interpretations of a particular *News at Ten* revealed a number of things:

1  We can assume very little about the meaning of a news item – a story that was intended to be about a politician's relations with his own party was, for example, decoded as a variety of quite different stories. News broadcasters, in fact, know remarkably little about what they are communicating to the outside world.

2  The ambiguity of the news is based on its narrative structure (or rather, lack of it). News 'stories' on TV are, most of the time, not stories at all. They are fragmented collections of information and images. Programmes with tight narrative structures – like *EastEnders* or, in a different way, *Blind Date*, will be far more successful at communicating an agreed set of meanings.

3  The images and words we select when we decode TV programmes will be based upon the meaning systems available in our heads. This, in

turn, forces us to construct different stories. For example, the regular *News at Ten* item detailing where jobs have been lost and found, to one viewer, was all about the shift from manufacturing industry in the north to service industries in the south, while another decoded it as an indicator that, although unemployment was still a problem, things were getting a little better. This happened because the two had quite different sets of experiences attached to the idea of unemployment, which allowed one to select the geographical information in the item, while the other focused on the numerical information. This interplay between the viewer and the television we can call *the process of decoding*.

This decoding process takes place within a whole social process. The meaning systems available to people are dependent upon social positions – whether in the family, at work or any other sets of social experiences. The meanings attached to 'Dirty Den' from *EastEnders* will depend upon our age, gender, experience of sexuality, experience of social class, experience of areas like the East End, experience of soap operas, experience of publicans, and so on. 'Dirty Den' will accordingly become hero, villain, sex symbol, small business entrepreneur, local boy made good, Jack the lad, or male chauvinist pig. This process has been described by David Morley as 'the person actively producing meanings from the restricted range of cultural sources which his or her position has allowed them access to' (Morley 1986).

The conditions wherein this takes place have been the subject of Morley's most recent TV audiences research. In *Family Television*, Morley has shifted his attention from what specific programmes mean, to people, to what he calls 'the *how* of television watching'. In short, people do not watch TV in research conditions. They watch it with their family, with friends, while having a conversation or eating breakfast. Moreover, television does not necessarily kill conversation, it can facilitate it. Peter Collett, a researcher who filmed people in their homes watching TV, puts it like this: 'Television is *what* people talk about, while it is on, as well as at work the next day. It buttresses social relationships in the sense that it gives people something to discuss. Often it provides a focus for people to talk about other things'.[10]

This leaves us with a television experience made up of four distinct but interactive components:

(i) the TV *programme*, with its set of narrative structures and its interplay of words and images;
(ii) the *viewer*, with her or his set of cultural codes/meaning systems;

163

(iii) *the viewing context* – how we watch TV, who with, what we do when we're watching it and what we do with those meanings afterwards;

(iv) *our social experience* through which we evolve meaning systems – part of this social experience being, of course, the experience of watching TV.

Research in the last decade has enabled us to understand this process. One of the next stages is to measure the effects of the television experience.

## Notes

1 Carl Hovland, 'Reconciling results derived from experimental and survey studies of attitude change', *The American Psychologist*, vol. 14 (1959).
2 Jay Blumler and Denis McQuail. 'The audience for election television', in Jeremy Tunstall (ed.), *Media Sociology*, London: Constable, 1970.
3 Gillian Dyer, *Advertising as Communication*, London: Methuen, 1982.
4 P. Hartman and C. Husband, 'The mass media and racial conflict', in Stan Cohen and Jock Young (eds), *The Manufacture of News*, London: Constable, 1983.
5 Elihu Katz, 'Mass communications research and the study of popular culture', *Studies in Public Communication*, vol. 2 (1959).
6 Denis McQuail, Jay Blumler, and Roger Brown, 'The television audience: a revised perspective', in Denis McQuail (ed.), *The Sociology of Mass Communications*, Harmondsworth: Penguin, 1972.
7 Katz, op. cit.
8 Blumler and McQuail, op. cit.
9 John Hartley, *Understanding News*, London: Methuen, 1982.
10 Quoted in Jane Root, *Open The Box*, London: Comedia, 1986.

## Further reading

Ang, Ien, *Watching Dallas*, London: Methuen, 1985.
Lewis, Justin, 'Decoding TV news', in Philip Drummond and Richard Paterson (eds), *Television in Transition*, London: British Film Institute, 1985.
Morley, David, *The 'Nationwide' Audience*, London: British Film Institute, 1980.
Morley, David, *Family Television: Cultural Power and Domestic Leisure*, London: Comedia, 1986.

# 12 TODAY'S TELEVISION, TOMORROW'S WORLD
## Patrick Hughes

## Introduction

It's growing harder to distinguish between television sets and computer terminals: they look increasingly similar, and have an increasing number of functions in common. As those similarities increase, we need to think *differently* about today's television, because it is outgrowing its original mission to 'educate, entertain and inform'. Changes in television are part of broader changes in the communications industry as a whole. These broader changes include the integration of press, broadcasting, telecommunications, and computers within new corporate structures; a reduction in the number of people who own the media; alterations to the range of films and television programmes available internationally; and a dilution in the various forms of regulation within which the media have traditionally operated.

Some people think that these broader changes are the direct and inevitable consequences of new technologies such as videodiscs, teletext, and satellites, and that changes occurring in society are determined by new technologies. 'Technological determinism', as this view is known, includes among its adherents those who assert that new cable systems and video machines will inevitably bring a greater variety of TV programmes. Other technological determinists – including the British government – say that the path out of recession requires comprehensive adoption of new communications technologies in factories and offices: the machines will save us! Technological determinism ignores the people, social institutions and political forces which are all part of innovation. It doesn't mention the intricate web of scientific, social, political, and economic factors at national and international levels. Instead, new technologies are seen as

165

random and inevitable results of a steamroller called 'Progress', and social change is reduced to merely a list of dates on which particular machines came onto the market.

This chapter argues that particular changes in communications technology aren't random and inevitable, but are part of *general* changes in the ownership and control of major sections of the national and international economy. It also argues that these general changes are the result of particular choices made by national governments and by international corporations. New television technologies such as video and satellites are like any technological innovations: they have the potential to reinforce the current structure and operation of their industry *and* also to challenge it. This chapter explains why this ambiguity is currently being resolved in ways which reinforce and assist the concentration of ownership and power, and indicates the potential in new television technologies to oppose it.

Many 'new' communications technologies merely enable international companies to do old jobs in new ways which help to concentrate and integrate the ownership and control of broadcasting – indeed of the whole of the cultural and communications industries – in a shrinking number of (corporate) hands. For instance, satellites enable television and film companies to do their old job of distributing programmes across the globe, but in new ways which undermine – for better or worse – national control over the availability of ideas.

The *real* innovation associated with these technologies is the integration of the machinery and companies involved in television with those involved in apparently diverse areas such as computers, telephones, and homeworking. Video, satellite, and cable help companies such as Philips, Thorn-EMI, and Warners to reorganize the ways in which knowledge, ideas, and culture are produced and distributed. A decreasing number of people (mainly white men) are attaining increased power to decide how, and in whose benefit, those industries should develop, and this changes the ways in which many people work. Communications satellites integrate telephones and video, for example, enabling major corporations to distribute clerical and administrative tasks globally to home-based data-processing workers, undermining the influence of the trade unions. Many of these corporations also dominate the film and television sectors.

### Domestic video

Domestic videocassette recorders (VCRs) are generally used to play prerecorded tapes which we buy or rent, and to 'time shift' – record

166

programmes as they are broadcast to watch later. Videodisc players (VDPs) are used to play prerecorded discs – rather like records. Indeed, the audio and video markets are related via the compact disc, a new type of audio disc which was developed from videodisc technology.

The market for domestic video is the outcome of global battles for world dominance between competing companies and their competing video 'systems' or 'formats'. After fifteen years, only two VCR 'systems' have survived: the 'VHS' system of the Japanese Victor Company (JVC), and the 'Betamax' system of the Sony company. The two competing videodisc 'systems' – the 'VHD' system from JVC, and 'Laservision' from Philips, are survivors of another battle, the most recent victim of which was the US-based multinational RCA. In April 1984, RCA discontinued its own VDP system – 'CED' or 'Selectavision' – on the grounds that its sales were unlikely to recover its development cost of more than $130m. To the victors comes increased power to determine what sort of material is available on video.

This hasn't, however, created an alternative source of 'programmes' to that of the broadcasting and cinema companies. The prerecorded material which is widely available on cassette and/or disc for sale and/or rental in the major high street video shops is mostly feature films which will already have been shown in cinemas and/or broadcast on television. This is because of collaboration by the video machine-makers (JVC, Sony, and Philips, plus the companies which manufacture their products under licence, such as Thorn-EMI) with major film and music companies (such as Twentieth Century Fox, CBS, Polydor) to carry only their material on precorded tapes and discs. Further, the high street video shops are dominated by companies which are themselves subsidiaries of the machine-makers – Radio Rentals and Visionhire (the subsidiaries of Thorn-EMI and Philips respectively), for example.

In summary: when 'market forces' cause the collapse of new media systems, the people who have bought them lose their money; the workers who manufacture them lose their jobs; and the winning companies increase their power over the market, which reduces the variety of views in the media and hinders attempts to expand it.

Allegedly, anyone can produce and distribute videos, records, films, and so on, with consumers deciding which become successful. In the cultural and communications industries, this notion of the supremacy of market forces has recently been counterposed with increasing force to the long tradition of 'regulation'. The notion of regulation has often been based on technical considerations: the limited number of frequencies available for broadcasters has required careful allocation by the state; and the requirement for a unified, national telecommunications system has required a monopoly which is run, or at least supervised, by the state. Adherents of regulation have also argued that those industries have a social or moral duty, expressed through such ideas as fairness, balance, shared costs, and universal access, and summarized in the phrase 'public service'.

However, it has been left to state officials and to executives in broadcasting and telecommunications to decide just what 'public service' means. These executives aren't directly accountable to the people who use the services, and national ownership of broadcasting and telecommunications systems hasn't given the population effective control over their operations. Consequently, the paternalism inherent in regulation may be seen as malevolent, however benevolent its intention. When the replacement of regulation by the free market is presented as increasing the choice of video programmes, for example, it becomes a very attractive proposition, and undermines the whole notion of social control through democratic structures.

However, the new video market is dominated by a handful of major companies, each accountable only to its shareholders – a majority of whom are companies and institutions like themselves. Do you think that a major distribution group such as Columbia-EMI-Warner launching 'Superman II' on video has the same resources of production, promotion, distribution and administration as, say, a neighbourhood Housing Aid Centre wishing to launch a video about the sale of Council Houses?

*Ambiguities in domestic video*

The ability to 'time-shift' programmes means a video-user can construct her/his own schedule of viewing, choosing not just what to watch but when and in what order. However, time-shifting doesn't affect the size of audiences – merely when we watch. More importantly, recording programmes for later viewing gives the video-user the oportunity to 'fast-forward' through the commercials. What price 'prime-time' television when a significant portion of the potential audience watches at a later date and avoids the commercials?

VCR's have also offered individuals and groups an opportunity to produce and distribute their own alternative material – either 'formal' programmes or 'scratch' videos. The Glasgow Media Group (a group of academics at Glasgow University) has used recordings of programmes to illustrate their analytical and critical points in a series of studies of television news and current affairs programmes. A set of videocassettes about the 1984 coal dispute as seen through the eyes of the National Union of Mineworkers (*The Miners' Campaign Videotapes*, available from Trade Films, Sheffield) were distributed internationally as part of the union's calls for support and solidarity. The ill-fated neighbourhood cable television stations of the 1970s used VCRs to provide alternative programmes to their audiences, and familiarized many non-broadcasters with basic television broadcasting equipment. Programmes produced for transmission by broadcasting or cable can be recorded onto cassette/disc to be shown and discussed in public arenas after their original transmission. The opportunities to comment publicly on programmes, at present given only to an elite on programmes like the BBC's *Did You See?*, could thus be given to a wider range of people in a diversity of contexts.

Those opportunities to challenge the pattern of dominance aren't always grasped in the most 'progressive' manner. For instance, pornographers have developed a new videocassette market, 'free' from the restrictions applied to the regulated and accountable broadcasters and, to a lesser extent, to the 'mainstream' feature film industry.

### Videotex and electronic publishing

Videotex is a general term, referring to any electronic system which makes computer-based information available via computer terminals or via specially adapted television sets. There are two main types; broadcast videotex and wired videotex.

Broadcast videotex, more commonly called teletext, transmits information via the airwaves alongside radio and television programmes. The user can only 'read' from a relatively limited number of 'pages' of information – s/he can't feed information into the system. The BBC's 'Ceefax', and the IBA's 'Oracle' services are teletext systems and, while part of the overall output of the BBC and IBA, they represent a clear example of today's television being used in a different way. Their growth has been recent and rapid: more than 1.5 million people in the UK use teletext's news pages, television programme guides, weather forecasts, sports reports, and programme subtitles for deaf people.

Wired videotex, more commonly called viewdata, transmits information via cable, such as a telephone line. Viewdata systems are 'interactive' – users can send information to the system's computer, as well as receive information from it. Viewdata is, therefore, a step further away from traditional uses of the television set. Readers in the UK may be familiar with the 'Prestel' viewdata system operated by British Telecom and transmitted via BT's network of telephone lines. It contains hundreds of thousands of TV screen-sized 'pages' of information, which users can search and read with a control pad linked to their telephone and television set/computer terminal. Its interactive capability allows Prestel subscribers to book theatre tickets by credit card, for instance.

Prestel is a *public* viewdata system – access to it is open to anyone willing to pay the running costs. There are also many *private* viewdata systems produced and sold by companies such as Rediffusion Computers and Philips Business Systems. Unlike Prestel, these systems are accessible only to specified (rich!) groups of users. Organizations using them include the Stock Exchange (financial information), travel agents such as Thomson Holidays (booking holidays), vehicle manufacturers such as British Leyland (running its dealer network and spares service), and chain stores such as Debenhams (communicating with its suppliers and its individual shops). More complex private viewdata systems are used in databases, which offer their subscribers access to large libraries of data and/or text. Some data/text will already have appeared in print, the rest may exist solely within the database. For convenience, we can call the combination of viewdata plus database systems electronic publishing.

## Ambiguities of videotext

With videotex systems, media companies (newspapers, radio and television stations, news agencies, and so on) can do their old job of providing information in 'new' ways without changing the nature and sources of that information. Electronic publishing is but one more chapter in a tradition of providing information through organizations which are centralized, large, and bureaucratic, and which all tend to become owned and controlled by a small group of people. Indeed, many electronic publishing companies already dominate other forms of publishing. Pergamon Infoline, for example, is owned by Robert Maxwell – publisher of Mirror Group newspapers, and a major shareholder in commercial broadcasting and cable television.

It could be argued that legislation might broaden the ownership and control of the major electronic publishing companies, increase accessibility, and ensure diversity in the material available. However, state restrictions on electronic publishing would be impossible to police, and the result would be 'electronic prohibition' in which only the rich would really be able to 'speak easy'! Videotex technology itself could challenge the dominance of the major electronic publishing companies by decentralizing the production and distribution of knowledge and ideas.

170

The growing interchangeability of televisions and microcomputers at home and at work, if combined with new public videotex systems, would make every potential 'reader' of videotex a potential publisher, too! The high-quality printers now becoming available extend that option to paper-based publishing, which would challenge the dominance of the press and broadcasters as 'mediators' of information.

People can already electronically 'publish' information through 'notice boards' of viewdata and electronic mail systems, although few can afford to. Few organizations make available details of their activities and policies through videotex systems. Public electronic publishing would raise the competitive pressure on them to do so, and lower the financial barriers by spreading the costs of the system among a multitude of users. This would enable the public to question in detail the information provided by campaigning groups, public organizations, political parties, trade unions, research organizations, companies, and so on; to make criticisms or comments; or to add further material. The 'mediation' of ideas by pundits, commentators, and experts could – if wished, and to varying degrees – be circumvented. Finally, decentralized electronic publishing could help the individuals and organizations currently ignored or misrepresented by the 'mainstream' media, and seeking redress, through a right of reply. Complainants could electronically publish their 'reply' on videotex, and elicit public support for a change in the editorial and scheduling decisions of the broadcasting and publishing organizations. While leaving untouched the 'public service' traditions of the broadcasting organizations, decentralized public electronic publishing could offer a continuing means of judging their adequacy.

## Satellite broadcasting

Satellites do one or both of two things: observation satellites (of which a particular form is the 'spy' satellite) observe events on earth, and report these to their controllers; communications satellites (of which a particular form is the telecommunications/television satellite) relay signals from one point on earth to another. Reception of satellite signals just requires a fixed dish aerial, and a 'black box' of electronics for decoding and amplifying the signals. Communications companies use satellites because a single satellite channel can carry much more communications traffic than can a terrestrial link such as a telephone cable. Television channels can therefore easily be distributed by satellite nationally or internationally to operators of local cable television systems via a large dish aerial. This use of a common or 'master' aerial by all the households subscribing to the cable system led to its description as Satellite Master Antenna Television (SMATV).

The first television channel to be distributed by satellite to local cable operators was established in the USA in 1975 by Time Inc. By 1983, a survey by the US National Cable Television Association identified fifty-one such channels, including two sports channels, four religious channels, three movie channels, a health channel, and a Spanish-language channel, together with satellite-distributed 'superstations' such as WGN-Chicago or WTBS-Atlanta, which specialize in entertainment and sports.

Europe, too has several SMATV services using the Eutelsat 1 F-1 medium-powered satellite:

- 'Sky': Murdoch's channel of general entertainment, received by more than 7 million cabled households throughout Europe (100,000 in the UK via Swindon Cable);
- 'TV-5': French Ministry of Foreign Affairs' French-language channel distributes 8 hours per day of programmes to 4.5 million cabled households, principally in France, Luxembourg, Belgium, and Switzerland;
- 'Teleclub': Swiss subscription-financed film channel;
- 'Filmnet': Netherlands-based subscription-financed film channel;
- 'RAI-1': the Italian public service broadcasters' channel.

Satellites with greater transmitting power can distribute television signals directly to people's homes via smaller (90 cm) dish aerials in a garden or on a roof – hence the term 'direct broadcasting by satellite' (DBS). Several DBS projects are now underway in Europe.

Britain's first DBS channel, Sky TV, owned by Rupert Murdoch's News International, began broadcasting in 1989, offering four channels:

- Sky Channel: general light entertainment;
- Sky News: round-the-clock news;
- Sky Movies: a film channel, which will become subscription based;
- Eurosport: sports coverage. Eurosport is owned by a consortium of European broadcasting companies.

Additional plans to launch a Disney channel fell through in May 1989. The Astra satellite, which broadcasts Sky, also carries four other channels – Screensport, Lifestyle, and The Children's Channel, owned by W. H. Smith, and MTV, the music video channel, owned by the Maxwell Entertainment Group.

In competition with Sky, British Satellite Broadcasting (BSB) is a consortium whose major shareholders include the Bond Corporation of

Australia, the Granada Group, Pearson, and Reed International. In 1989 BSB planned to establish three channels:

- The Movie Channel: a film channel funded by subscriptions;
- Now: all day news, sport and current affairs;
- Galaxy: general light entertainment;

and as this book went to press they were also hoping to introduce Power (a music channel) and a separate sports channel. But financial and development problems led to the postponement of their launch until Spring 1990.

In each case, consumers must add the cost of the dish to the cost of any subscription services they choose. This cost (around £200), along with early problems in distributing dishes to the high street, led Sky to revise its estimated viewing figures radically, early in 1989, just before its launch. Even this downward vision of 1.15 million households by January 1990 was considerably beyond Saatchi & Saatchi's prediction that only 418,000 British households would have dishes by the end of 1989. Competition between Sky and BSB will be intense, and many commentators believe that the two services (which utilize incompatible broadcast technologies) cannot both survive.

*Ambiguities in satellite broadcasting*

The problems surrounding satellites tend to overwhelm their ambiguities. Those problems are due partly to the technology of satellite transmission itself, which was developed to overcome the barriers to communications erected by national governments; and partly to the classic conflict between 'nationalism' and 'internationalism'. The ambiguities of satellite broadcasting, and the room for manoeuvre, lie in that conflict.

Satellite broadcasting can bring enormous educational benefits. The example frequently given is India, where thousands of villages have been receiving agricultural and health education programmes delivered via satellites since 1975. However, satellite broadcasting could increase the threat of 'cultural imperialism' – the undermining of cultural and political values of poor countries by those of richer and more powerful ones. This process has been happening for some years, based on the international distribution of relatively cheap cultural products such as films and television programmes, mainly produced in the USA and western Europe. These have been imported by existing (terrestrial) television services in many Third World countries, unable to afford the cost of producing many programmes which represent their national cultures and traditions. When they import such programmes, they also import their cultural and political values. Since those same programme-producing companies now also own and operate satellite services, there are fears that satellite broadcasting services could further damage and/or exploit the culture and politics of countries receiving them.

A 'nationalist' response to those fears could be to erect national barriers to protect a nation's culture, politics, and way of life from being undermined and/or exploited. For instance, some countries, such as Sweden, have decided to ban commercials on domestic and imported television programmes. However, 'exporting' television programmes by satellite undermines those national restrictions, since commercials need only be approved in the country of transmission. The satellite services received by Swedish viewers included commercials by overseas companies, which led Swedish companies to press for advertising on domestic (terrestrial) television to enable them, so they say, to compete effectively with those overseas companies. (The drive to spread television advertising relates to its cost. Two typical 30-second commercials on UK commercial television can cost approximately £120,000, and the greater audiences reached by satellite reduce the cost per viewer of producing commercials.)

A nationalist view can, however, prevent the population of a particular country from understanding that the problems they face may well be due to forces beyond the control of one nation, and are indeed shared by people in other countries. The problems posed to individual national governments and cultures by satellite broadcasting are clearly international: the satellites themselves are owned and operated by international companies on an international scale. The problems posed by satellite broadcasting aren't restricted to poor countries; concern has also been expressed in several industrialized countries at their cultural implications. French politicians were alarmed by proposals from RTE in Luxemburg to transmit programmes by satellite across Europe; other European governments have expressed horror at the thought of US-based corporations beaming 'Coca-Cola culture' by DBS into their nations' homes.

Many of those expressions of concern are, however, nationalistic. They denigrate the culture and politics of the country in which satellite services originate (usually the USA or western Europe) and compare them unfavourably with those of the country of reception, implying that certain cultures are inherently 'better' or 'worse' than others. An internationalist response would focus instead on how satellite television is owned and controlled. It would explain that threats to particular national cultures are due to the lack of democratic accountability in the ownership and operation of satellites, and in the allocation of their orbits. The problems aren't other cultures, they are the international companies in the cultural and communications industries.

Current use of satellites poses problems other than just 'cultural' ones, and these, too, illustrate the need for an internationalist perspective. Satellite communication makes it easier for companies to transfer clerical and administrative work to Third World countries. (They are following the example of manufacturing companies which use new technologies to simplify component manufacture, reducing the need for highly trained staff, and enabling them to shift their operations to the cheaper and less-organized workforces of the Third World.) The leading firms of printers in the City of London are buying satellite links that enable them to produce financial documents simultaneously in London and New York; some 'offshore' typesetting and proofreading is sent from London to India and other countries via airlines. An increase in satellite communications, and a reduction in its cost, will mean that this sort of distributed office work will increase. A nationalist response would clearly be inadequate.

Since satellite technology can integrate 'culture' (television) with 'economics' (distributed office work), an internationalist response must do the same. It must be more than some form of 'snobbery' confined to the concerns of an individual nation's cultural elite. Its base must be broader than just particular workplaces. It must recognize that the broadly white, male, and metropolitan domination of satellite operations poses particular problems to people of different races, to women, and to non-industrial countries and cultures.

People in many countries have challenged their national media's dominant representations of working-class people and institutions, of women, of black people, and of the concerns of each of those groupings. Satellite television means that those challenges must become international, linking and integrating national campaigns. They must also be integrated with an increase in the international responses made by many workers in international companies through their trade unions to the employment and investment policies of these companies. Neither form of response would in itself be adequate; new multinational democratic organizations are needed to counter the policies of the international companies.

An 'internationalist' approach to satellite broadcasting is, however, unlikely to be developed in the near future. Many Third World countries fear that by the time they can afford to launch their own satellites, all the prime orbits will have been allocated to satellites from the richer countries. Third World fears have been heightened by the refusal of those rich countries to contemplate any regulation of allocations, preferring instead to rely on the first-come-first-served basis that enables them to exploit their technological lead over the Third World.

## Cable and homeworking

Cable systems were originally established to improve the quality of radio and television signals in areas where hills, tall buildings, and so on caused interference with domestic reception. From a tall mast aerial in a prominent position, the operator of a cable system directs a high-quality broadcast signal to a network of cables passing by a number of households (a form of MATV). Those living near a trunk route in this network can usually be connected to it for a flat monthly fee.

In the UK, cable companies have until recently been restricted to relaying broadcast television and radio channels. However, the introduction of very high frequency (VHF) broadcasting made it easier to receive high-quality BBC and IBA signals in virtually all of the UK's populated areas. Subscriptions to cable systems dwindled; why pay a cable company when you can get everything it provides merely by sticking an aerial out of your home? Consequently, the cable companies have lobbied successive governments for permission to provide services other than just relayed broadcasts. In some other countries, cable subscribers can receive many more channels. Cable subscribers in the USA receive relayed broadcasts of television from the three networks (NBC, ABC, CBS) plus other services including locally originated programmes, public access channels, and special satellite-distributed services such as:

- Cable News Network (CNN): a 24-hour news channel;
- Entertainment and Sports Programming Network (ESPN);
- Music Television (MTV): a 24-hour pop music video channel.

(The providers of those special service channels raise revenue through a levy on the operator, or through selling advertising time on their channel, or both.) That whole package is called 'basic cable'. Its cost is met by the operator of each local cable system through the subscription fee (around $15 a month) paid by each household receiving the cable service.

As well as 'basic cable', cable operators in the USA usually offer a second tier of services, known as pay TV or subscription TV. The subscriber pays a further fee for each pay TV channel s/he chooses to receive, and each pay TV channel is 'scrambled' so that only those

176

subscribers who pay the cable operator for a descrambling device can receive them. Two of the best-known pay TV channels are Showtime, and Time Inc.'s Home Box Office (HBO). Each shows feature films, with no commercial breaks, in contrast to network television.

In 1982, the British government's Information Technology Advisory Panel (ITAP), in its *Report on Cable Systems*, recommended that private companies should be encouraged to establish new, high-capacity local cable systems, Each would have monopoly control over a minimum of thirty different channels, including interactive videotex services such as home shopping and home banking.

The ITAP proposals – like the 1983 Cable Act which they spawned – contained three weaknesses, which led the government's cable policy to collapse. First, they are unlikely to provide the predicted plethora of 'special interest' channels. Commercially oriented cable systems seek to offer advertisers the maximum audiences for the maximum time. Consequently, any 'specialist' channel (such as cultural, ethnic, or access programming) must match the audiences – and thus the advertisers – of 'mainstream' channels, or close – as did CBS's 'culture' cable channel in the USA. On the other hand, what is the attraction to potential subscribers of 'mainstream' programming/video available elsewhere?

Secondly, there is no free market in cable, and so any new market is likely to be dominated by already-existing major cable companies. Establishing cable systems, and providing the services on them, requires enormous financial and organizational resources available only to corporations with large resources drawn from other activities including other sectors of the cultural and communications industries. Hence the dominance of companies such as Time Inc., owners of Home Box Office, and Warner-Amex (a joint venture between Warner Communications and American Express), owners (until its sale in 1985 to Viacom) of the Satellite Entertainment Company, which controlled The Movie Channel, MTV, and the Nickelodeon children's service. The group also owns and operates a number of cable systems in the USA, drawing on Warner's film library and production facilities.

Thirdly, equating interactive services and new cable systems is misplaced. Many interactive services are already available, albeit in an uncoordinated fashion, without needing to subscribe to a new cable system. For instance, remote metering of electricity usage was launched by Thorn-EMI in 1982; Prestel and other viewdata services can provide home shopping; and various schemes are in operation to provide home banking services. Since they're already available elsewhere, why pay to receive them via cable?

Depite those weaknesses, the ITAP proposals became law for two reasons. First, the government wanted to open the hitherto-protected UK cable market to competition from communications corporations based overseas (mainly in the USA). Its 1983 Cable Act was meant to expose the stagnating UK cable companies to new competition in the provision of new cable technology and the new products and services to be available through it.

The second, more compelling, reason may appear to have nothing to do with today's television. Restructuring the UK cable industry matches the government's long-term strategy of assisting private capital to weaken the distinction between home, work, and commerce, and move towards an 'information society'.

While today's television isn't the focus of that strategy to create an information society, it is certainly affected by it. As part of that strategy, the government has encouraged the growth of a strong domestic information technology industry (1982 was the government's 'Information Technology Year'). Its telecommunications legislation altered the UK telecommunications market: it reduced the traditional domination by BT and the handful of companies (such as Plessey and GEC) manufacturing its equipment by exposing it to 'market forces', – that is, foreign-based multinational companies. Meanwhile, private capital has altered the operations of UK telecommunications by establishing Mercury as a competitor to British Telecom (BT), and by privatizing BT itself. The role of the new cable systems in that information society would be to provide an 'electronic grid'. It would connect with and complement British Telecom's and Mercury's national telecommunications networks, carry data and information cheaply and quickly around the country, and link with similar networks overseas.

ITAP was aware that this particular government wouldn't provide an 'electronic grid' as a public service, in the way that previous governments had provided the roads, railways, gas, and electricity infrastructure. It proposed – and the government agreed through its 1983 Cable Act – that the grid's spread across the country should be 'market-led' or 'entertainment-led': new cables should be laid by new private companies responding to demand for entertainment services from potential customers. The government was to minimize the constraints of broadcasting policy and technical requirements which might interfere with investment in this 'free' market.

The creation of the legislative basis of an 'information society' has accompanied changes in multinational communications corporations, based on the integration of technologies – and thus operations –

178

previously associated with different companies. Their domination of the cultural and communications industries has thus increased such that they can influence our lives at home and at work. An example is Philips, a multinational based in the Netherlands. Philips' agreements with film companies concerning its 'Laservision' videodisc system influences our choice of viewing on this new form of television; its Business Systems division influences the nature, pace, and conditions of our work in new forms of 'high tech' office; and its UK cable systems (through its subsidiary Electronic Rentals Group) influence how we spend our money in new forms of banking and shopping from home. Another example is Robert Maxwell's Pergamon Group, owners of the *Daily Mirror, Sunday Mirror,* and *Sunday People.* Its recent development has been similar to that of Philips. In 1984, Mirror Group Newspapers integrated Pergamon's interests in paper-based publishing with its interests in cable, paying a bargain £11 million for Rediffusion's entire interests in cable systems. These interests included:

- a franchise to operate a new, high-capacity cable system in Guildford, to add to the Mirror Group's existing interest in Clyde Cablevision's new cable franchise in Glasgow;
- an interest in The Entertainment Channel;
- a network of 'old', lower-capacity cable systems in thirty-six towns – the most extensive in the country.

This meant that Pergamon could challenge the Sky satellite entertainment channel owned by Rupert Murdoch's News International, the Mirror Group's press rival. It enabled Pergamon to expand its electronic publishing interests, and thereby strengthen its involvement in data-processing and 'high tech' office work. Finally, it offered Pergamon an entry to home-based shopping (and, who knows, home-based teletex Bingo!).

In broadcasting, market forces – in the form of increased use of advertising – are being used to weaken the principles of public accountability and public service. The government's Peacock Committee recommended that part of the BBC's revenue could come from advertising on Radio 1, Radio 2, and BBC local radio in whole or in part. Moreover, it suggested that commercial television could be sold off to the highest financial bidder, rather than awarded to companies judged to be proposing the highest-quality service.

In the projected expansion of the cable industry, the public service tradition of broadcasting is to be abandoned in favour of competition between new, small businesses. However, the innovatory, alternative, pluralistic programming which such a scenario might be expected to produce is unlikely to arise. Major communications companies already dominate the shareholding structures of the first of the new cable companies. These include British Telecom (Merseyside Cablevision, Swindon Cable); Mirror Group Newspapers (Glasgow's Clyde Cablevision); and Thorn-EMI (shareholder in Coventry Cable). The major programme-providers are companies that already dominate other sectors of the culture and communications industries such as cinema, records, and the press. Their priorities and objectives are now dominating the cable sector. Since the 1983 Cable Act, the 'old' local cable systems need no longer relay broadcast signals. Consequently, many of them now transmit a service of four to six television channels providing mainly feature films from major distributors.

The handful of 'new', higher-capacity cable systems established since that Act provide a basic package of the four broadcast television channels, accompanied by one or more of the following:

- The Entertainment Channel: a film channel supported by Paramount, MGM/United Artists, Universal, Plessey and Rank-Trident;
- Premiere: a film channel supported by Thorn-EMI, Goldcrest Films, Twentieth Century Fox, HBO, Showtime/The Movie Channel, Columbia, and Warner;
- Sky Channel: 'general entertainment' delivered by the Sky satellite, owned by Satellite Television plc, a subsidiary of News International;
- Music Box: a pop music channel led by Thorn-EMI and Virgin, and distributed throughout Europe by Sky satellite;
- Lifestyle: led by W. H. Smith (backers of the Consumer Channel and owners of the 'Our Price' chain of record shops);
- others, including Screensport, The Children's Channel and The Arts Channel.

Instead of a thriving source of innovation and diversity, the 'new' UK cable systems will be the province of multinational corporations, unfettered by anything other than residual state regulation. (The Cable Authority established under the 1983 Cable Act is tellingly referred to as an 'oversight' body!).

The government's Spring 1984 Budget accelerated those inbuilt tendencies towards monopoly, because it phased out tax allowances on capital expenditure – such as the construction of new cable systems. This increased the capital needs of new companies wishing to enter the cable market, already struggling to meet their capital targets, even when subsidized through tax allowances.

180

Since 1982, most public debate has accepted the assumption that 'cable' means 'cable TV'. Little attention has been paid to the implications of an electronic grid for the government's goal of an 'information society', and in particular the opportunities it offers to employers to create a new generation of white-collar homeworkers. Administrative and clerical work can already be done at home with a computer terminal (or a modified television) and a British Telecom telephone line to employers' premises. Companies such as ICL, Rank-Xerox, and F International have for some time operated such electronic white-collar homeworking. Electronics manufacturers such as Commodore and Rediffusion have produced computers ('work stations') which can be used at home and at work. However, the present high rents of telecommunications links make white-collar homeworking cost-effective only to employers of highly-paid professional and managerial staff. A cheap 'electronic grid' would enable employers to shift large areas of information processing work – such as secretarial/text processing, data entry, order processing, and even process-control in manufacturing – from the office to the home.

Working at home saves time and money on travel, and gives more flexibility in how and when to do the day's tasks. Hence its popularity with middle managers, and with women who have children but inadequate child-care facilities. However, it isolates workers thus reducing their ability to act collectively to protect their pay and conditions of work. It also means that individual workers, not the employer, pay the costs of lighting, heating, and maintaining their workplace.

This may seem far removed from a discussion of today's television and of the 'cable revolution', until we remember that alongside the development of such an electronic grid would be the continuing trend towards monopoly in the provision of news, entertainment, and information across the whole of the culture and communications industries. For many people, the 'information society' could mean a future in which a few corporations dominate their working lives and their leisure lives via a video screen. For those corporations, and for those white-collar homeworkers, today's 'television' may well become tomorrow's world.


## Further reading

Particular changes in the structures, operations, and products of the companies in the culture and communications industries are reported as they happen in the general business and financial media such as *The Financial Times*, *The Economist*, *Fortune*, and *Business Week*. There are also the magazines and journals specializing in reporting and commenting on these industries, including *Broadcast* and *New Media Markets* in the UK, the US magazine *Channels of Communication*, and *Electronics Today International* in Australia. For a discussion of the prospects of satellite television, see Richard Collins, 'The prognosis for satellite television in the UK', *Space Policy*, February 1989.

More substantial background reading would include the following:

Forester, T. (ed.), *The Information Technology Revolution*, Oxford: Blackwell, 1985.

Mattelart, A., Delcourt, X., and Mattelart, M., *International Image Markets*, London: Comedia, 1984.

Murphy, B., *The World Wired Up: Unscrambling the New Communications Puzzle*, London: Comedia, 1983.

Turney, J., (ed.), *Sci-Tech Report*, London: Pluto, 1984.

# INDEX

192